Management, How To

A Concise Guide to Understanding Management Skills, Styles, and Systems, and How to Use them in the Real World.

By:

Joseph A. Neville Ph.D.

Copyright © 2017 by Joseph A. Neville Ph.D.
All rights reserved. This book or any portion thereof may not be reproduced or used in any manner whatsoever without the express written permission of the publisher except for the use of brief quotations in a book review.

Printed in the United States of America

First Printing, 2017

ISBN 978-1979813310

About the Author

Joseph has spent the past several years studying the field of business administration and management, and has worked in both the profit and non-profit fields. Joseph has earned a Ph.D. in Business Administration, Management, is a Certified Master Coach, and holds Bachelor and Masters degrees in Psychology. He applies his knowledge of psychology and coaching to help individuals and businesses reach their goals, from small town shops to major multinational corporations.

Table of Contents

CHAPTER 1 1

WHAT IS MANAGEMENT? 1

    THE FOUR TASKS OF MANAGEMENT 2
    LEADING 2
    ORGANIZATION: 4
    PLANNING: 5
    CONTROLLING: 6
    MANAGEMENT BELIEFS: THEORY X AND THEORY Y 8
    MANAGEMENT STYLES 12
        The Avoider: 13
        The Accommodator: 16
        The Competitor: 18
        The Intimidator: 21
        The Compromiser: 23
        The Collaborator: 25

CHAPTER 2 28

COMMUNICATION 28

HOW DO I COMMUNICATE EFFECTIVELY AS A MANAGER?
.... 28

    3 TYPES OF COMMUNICATION 30
        Written Communication: 31
    HOW TO IMPROVE YOUR SPEAKING ABILITIES IN 5 STEPS 41
        Non-Verbal Communication 43

CHAPTER 3 52

ETHICS AND CREDIBILITY 52

HOW CAN I BE AN ETHICAL MANAGER? 52

    HOW TO IMPROVE WORK ETHICS IN 4 STEPS. 60

CHAPTER 4 62

INTERVIEWING 62

HOW DO I INTERVIEW PEOPLE, AND KNOW WHO TO
HIRE? 62

    Interviewing Strategies 63
    Interviewing skills 70
    Body language 72
    How to conduct interviews in 4 Phases 74

CHAPTER 5 80

TEAMS 80

HOW DO I MANAGE EFFECTIVE TEAMS? 80

    WHAT ARE TEAMS? 81
        Types of team members 83
        The leader: 84
        The implementer 84
        The thinker: 85
        The contributor: 85
        The builder: 85
        The inquisitor: 85
        The outsider: 86
    HOW TO PICK TEAMS IN 6 STEPS 86

CHAPTER 6 90

    Vroom's Expectancy Theory 91
    HOW TO MEET EMPLOYEE EXPECTATIONS IS 3 STEPS. 93
    Adam's Equity Theory 96
    HOW TO IMPROVE EQUITY AND MEET EMPLOYEE EXPECTATIONS IN
    4 STEPS. 99
    WHERE DOES MOTIVATION COME FROM? 101
        Internal Motivation 104
        External motivation 109
    HOW TO MOTIVATE EMPLOYEES IN 4 STEPS. 112

CHAPTER 7 116

DELEGATING RESPONSIBILITY 116

HOW CAN I BE EFFECTIVE AT DELEGATION? 116

    How to delegate responsibility in 5 steps............ 118

CHAPTER 8 124

MANAGING CHANGE............ 124

HOW DO I MANAGE CHANGE EFFECTIVELY?............ 124

    Anticipated changes *126*
    Unanticipated changes *132*
    How to manage change with 5 skills. *136*

CHAPTER 9 147

CONFLICT RESOLUTION 147

HOW DO I EFFECTIVELY RESOLVE CONFLICTS? 147

    How to resolve conflicts in 5 steps 148

CHAPTER 10 157

FIRING 157

WHO DO I FIRE, AND HOW DO I DO IT? 157

    How to fire someone in 4 strategic stages 158

APPENDIX – SYSTEMS 167

    How to improve your speaking abilities in 5 Steps 167
    How to improve work ethics in 4 steps. 168
    How to conduct interviews in 4 Phases *169*
    How to pick teams in 6 steps 171
    How to meet employee expectations is 3 steps. 172
    How to improve equity and meet employee expectations in 4 steps. 173
    How to motivate employees in 4 steps. 174
    How to delegate responsibility in 5 steps 176
    How to manage change with 5 skills. *177*
    How to resolve conflicts in 5 steps 180
    How to fire someone in 4 strategic stages 182

REVIEW REQUEST 186

REFERENCES 187

Introduction

Studying management may be as exciting to some people as watching grass grow. I must admit, I have read a great deal of material on management that nearly put me to sleep because it was terribly uninteresting. I knew that I needed to read and learn the material, but struggled with connecting the information to the real world. I knew that I was learning something about management that should be useful to my career, but seeing how the concepts would be utilized in my day to day life was not easy. I thought that there had to be a better way to learn these concepts. That is how *Management, How To* was born.

Management, How To takes complex management concepts and presents them in an engaging way that not only allows for learning about management to be interesting, but also sparks a bit of excitement about the potential to instantly apply these skills to your management repertoire. *Management, How To* is different from other books on management in that it not only provides you with the technical knowledge of management concepts, but also offers real world examples and dialogs that help to bring the ideas to life.

On top of the practical examples *Management, How To* delivers easily applicable systems related to each concept that you can implement into your management practice today! These systems have been designed to allow managers to quickly and easily recall and utilize management skills with confidence.

Most management books provide information about topics, but do not present it in a way that allows readers to remember what they just read. *Management, How To* solves this problem by presenting material to readers in different ways and from different angles which makes the information memorable. To achieve this *Management, How To* incorporates technical information, psychological principles, and coaching methodology to engage learning.

So, who is this book for? When I set out to write *Management, How To*, I wanted to create a resource that could be used by anyone who is involved in management; from universities, major multi-national corporations, small businesses, non-profit organizations, to government agencies. The college student studying business or management will be able to absorb a wealth of knowledge from this book that will be useful throughout his or her career. The new manager will be able to learn about implementing management concepts and understanding different management styles. The seasoned manager will be able to gain perspective on concepts they have been using for many years by looking at them through a new lens. *Management, How To* is truly unique in that it brings clarity to concepts that people in all levels of management will find beneficial.

How to use this book? This book should be used as a tool for learning about management styles, skills, and systems, and how to use them in the real world. You can read the book cover to cover or jump from chapter to chapter to learn about management in the manner that best suits your individual preferences. *Management, How To* lends itself as a resource that you can go back to again and again whenever you see fit.

Now, are you ready to get started?

Chapter 1
What is Management?

"A good manager is best when people barely know that he exists. Not so good when people obey and acclaim him. Worse when they despise him."

- ***Lao Tzu***

What is management? In the truest sense of its meaning management is a process by which leaders within organizations attempt to achieve goals by utilizing the resources available to them. So, what does this mean? This means that managers take on the task of accomplishing goals for companies by looking at what they have available, such as materials and personnel, and making choices on how to achieve the highest probability of success for their organizations.

Managers lead.

Managers organize.

Managers plan.

Managers take control.

The Four Tasks of Management

These are the four primary tasks of management. Each of these tasks plays a pivotal role in the overall functionality of businesses. To be an effective manager, individuals must possess skills and become proficient at them.

Leading: Managers must lead employees to be the best possible versions of themselves. Leadership refers to the notion that an individual has influence over others. Managers take on this role when they put on the shoes of the boss. No single factor is more important than the leadership abilities of individuals seeking to become managers. Skill and talent are extremely important but, those who do not possess leadership abilities will likely not become effective managers. This isn't to say that individuals cannot learn leadership skills and improve upon their management abilities. With hard work and dedication, as anything else, people can develop leadership skills and grow in the role as a manager.

Take for instance Abraham Lincoln. Throughout his pursuits of public office, he lost nearly as many elections as he won.

August 1832 – loses race for Illinois House of Representatives seat.

August 1834 – wins seat in Illinois House of Representatives.

December 1838 – loses bid for speaker of the Illinois House of Representatives.

August 1846 – wins election to Congress.

November 1854 – wins seat in Illinois House of Representatives.

February 1855 – loses bid for Senate seat.

November 1858 – loses bid for Senate seat again.

November 1860 – wins election as President.

November 1864 – wins reelection as President.[2]

Despite his losses Lincoln was persistent in his goals of winning public offices. He never gave up on his dreams to be a political leader no matter how many times he faced adversity. Through all those losses Lincoln was able to learn new skills and strategies to implement the next time he ran for office. He utilized his losses as time to learn how to become a better leader.

As a manager you may not face quite as much adversity as Lincoln, but you can learn from his example, and understand that though you may be lacking in one area or another there is always room for improvement if you have the heart to learn what you need. Leaders are by no means perfect people. They're just people who are placed in a position where others look to them for guidance. Managers are placed in roles that put them in a position to direct the efforts of employees, or to lead them.

The concept of leading in management is quite different than what Abraham Lincoln faced however, managers in today's organizations must be able to effectively lead employees to create an atmosphere of productivity. To achieve this, managers must utilize the other skills mentioned above: organizing, planning, and controlling.

Organization: Organization allows managers to be more efficient in their duties. Having an effective organizational system for managing the day-to-day tasks, and goals, of managers allows them to be more efficient in their usage of time, and allows them to have flexibility enough to meet challenges that arise.

Organization for a manager leads to success, disorganization leads to chaos. I once had a manager who I really liked personally. She was very effective at listening and collaborating with the team to come up with solutions which we will get to in *Chapter 2*. However, when I went into her office she had stacks of files and papers all around the room to the point where you could only walk to two chairs and sit down, nothing else. I could never understand, even as a fresh graduate, how she could possibly know where things were, or how she could find something if you asked her. This quickly became apparent as I settled into my job. I was required to give her reports and documents on a regular basis. I learned that if I wanted access to these reports and documents I had to make copies for myself before giving her the originals. She never missed any meetings, she always had time to talk, and I could always feel that she genuinely cared about me as an employee and as a person, but her organizational skills in her office affected her ability to be efficient. I learned a lot from her about being a good manager, and I learned a lot about how not to manage. Effective organization makes all the difference in a manager's ability to quickly and efficiently get things done.

Planning: There is an old adage, typically associated with Benjamin Franklin, that says if you fail to plan you plan to fail. This has been quoted throughout business literature so many times that it begins to lose its importance. The simplicity of the statement is also its strength. Planning is the foundation of business growth. Without planning businesses will remain stagnant and will either remain where they are or begin to slide down on the evolutionary life-cycle of organizations. Managers who do not take planning seriously, potentially doom their companies to failure.

To plan effectively, managers need to understand where their company is currently, and where they would like to see the company go. Once they understand where the company is they can collaborate with everyone involved and create goals for their company's future. Once they have goals in place they can dig into the feasibility of each of the steps necessary. Planning each step along the way may be an arduous task, but will promote the greatest potential for success. Effective planning helps managers to lead their teams through the change process, and gives them the direction they need to guide their employees along the path of success.

Controlling: The term controlling may seem harsh, as if managers need to control each and every movement an employee makes. That's not what's being said. To be effective, managers must be able to monitor the progression of work being done by employees, as well as keep track of the advancement of goals. By keeping tabs on how the day-to-day operations are functioning managers are able to attain a level of control over their sphere of influence. This is the concept of control that is of utmost importance to managers.

Control can be achieved in a variety of ways. Managers essentially have five styles, or approaches, of handling these kinds of situations, which will be discussed later in this chapter. Whichever style each manager chooses to incorporate has influence over how control is achieved. For example, when I was working on my bachelor's degree I worked for a company installing low-voltage wiring in new homes. My boss was a very nice man, but he feared conflicts with people and avoided them at all costs. He was a very trusting supervisor and allowed me to get the work done without micro-management. He would simply tell me an address, when it needed to be finished, and I went to work whenever it was convenient for me. Mostly I would go in at night after classes and after all the tradesmen had left. Often I would leave work as soon as I finished and would have a quarter hour on my time card. Eventually my boss told me he did not like to deal with quarter hours and asked me not to put them on my time card. I thought that it was a little strange but didn't really mind. So, my plan then was to save the quarter hours until I had a full hour, or if I finished at three quarters of an hour and had a quarter hour from the day before I simply added this onto my time card. I thought this was a good idea at the time. When I asked my boss if this was okay and he said yes, but I found out later that he really didn't like that either, which led to a lot of ambiguity and misunderstanding.

This was a powerful lesson I learned on the importance of communication, but that's a subject for *Chapter 2.*

Management Beliefs: Theory X and Theory Y

Now that we've covered the four main skills of managers let's explore management styles. In the late 1950s a researcher by the name of Douglas McGregor began to see a trend in how managers viewed their employees. McGregor realized that managers fit into one of two belief systems, or categories. The first system believes that employees are inherently bad or lazy. He called this Theory X. The second system believes that employees are inherently good and want to do well. He called this Theory Y.[3]

Theory X: Theory X managers hold a view of employees that consists of mostly negative aspects such as a disinterest in work, an unwillingness to put forth effort, and laziness. This concept is just as prevalent in today's workplace as it was when McGregor discovered it. Many managers hold the view that their employees do only the bare minimum of work they are required to do to receive their paychecks.

Is this an unfair assessment? Maybe, but maybe not. Many employees would rather do pretty much anything other than work. In fact, I would bet that it's safe to say that most employees would rather be doing something else with their time. But, to earn a living, employees must go to work, and do the tasks they were hired to do.

Theory X managers believe in the old Spanish proverb which says: to not watch your workman is to lose your money. These managers feel as though their employees do not care about their jobs nor do they feel any kind of loyalty to their company. They simply come to work, do the minimal amount possible, and leave with no positive regard for their workplace. Managers who believe this about their employees have no hope for the existence of an optimistic work environment to exist.

Theory Y: On the other side of the coin are Theory Y managers. Theory Y managers hold an overly optimistic view that all their employees are inherently good, and only want what's best for the company. You might think that this is a naïve view but, it is quite common amongst managers today.

Theory Y managers want to believe that only good intentions come from employees and that their efforts are always aimed at improving the organization. These managers also believe that employees genuinely enjoy coming to work and are more than capable of completing the tasks to which they are assigned. Theory Y managers value their employees and respect their thoughts, feelings, and opinions. These managers believe that encouraging the positive feelings employees have about their workplace will create an environment of loyal team members who constantly strive to do their best.

It seems like a good idea to think that everyone is a good person and that they only want to better themselves to make the company a better place. However, employees have motivational factors that influence their decisions and drive to do well in such a wide array of aspects that it is quite impossible to lump all employees into one category or the other. Employees are too diverse to categorize in such a way.

Unfortunately, McGregor passed away shortly after publishing his work about theory X and theory Y. Although he was unable to continue the research himself he envisioned that managers would look at these theories, decide which theory they believed, and try to form an understanding of how to be a better manager.

Which Theory?

So, which is the most effective approach? Well, the simple answer is neither. Managers who think only think negatively about their employees will only find negative behaviors on which to base their opinion. Managers who only think positively about their employees' motivation tend to overlook when negative behaviors arise.

The most effective approach is to understand that each employee is unique, therefore, his or her circumstances are also diverse. Managers need to look at each employee and understand what motivates him or her, to gain a perspective on employee motivation, which is covered in *Chapter 7*. By learning about Theory X and Theory Y you can decide for yourself which blend between the two theories is most appropriate for your work environment.

For example, you could follow the standard by believing that employees are 80% good and 20% bad. By bad, I am being facetious and simply mean that they may not completely agree with everything that goes on within a company, but are mostly positive about their jobs. If the 80/20 rule doesn't apply to your belief structure about employees, you can adjust it as you see fit such as 90/10, 95/5 or, even 99/1.

The ratio to which you apply positive attributes to employees depends on your personal situation, but does not mean that it must stay in its' original place. As time goes on, and as you grow in your managerial skill, you may be able to slide the positive aspect of your beliefs further up the scale. This is also greatly affected by the management style you choose to implement in your day-to-day management practice.

Management Styles

As you can see from looking at Theory X and Theory Y the beliefs that managers have about employees may affect how they approach their management style. Managers choose, knowingly or not, to implement a specific style based on experiences they have had in the past, as well as experiences in their present. When I say knowingly or not, I mean many managers have not taken the time to reflect on why they choose to act a certain way in management situations.

A manager may know what seems to be working for him or her, but may not understand where their motivation comes from to utilize a particular management style. Understanding why you implement a specific management style will help you grow as a manager and develop your management skills. When broken down to their core form, there are six major management styles which I have named: the Avoider, the Accommodator, the Competitor, the Intimidator, the Compromiser, and the Collaborator. Each of these styles is unique in how, and where, it should be implemented. Also, each style represents a specific set of behaviors that managers display, whether they know it or not.

In this section we will explore the six management styles and how each style shows up in the behavior of managers.

The Avoider: This type of manager attempts to avoid conflict at all costs. They look past the situation and hope that everything will work out in the end. The Avoider goes to great lengths to overlook the need for action in situations that he or she feels may turn into a conflict. This tends to be pretty much everything in the field of management.

The Avoider assumes that problems will either fix themselves or that someone else will take care of them. This can lead to a great amount of ambiguity and confusion. This type of manager can be quite indecisive and unassertive. Take for example the boss I referred to earlier in this chapter who avoided talking to me rather than expressing what he felt. He was an Avoider. Rather than come to me and have a conversation about what was going on he felt as though avoiding the situation would fix the problem. However, avoiding the real issue only made things worse and caused him to feel upset about a situation that could have easily been cleared up.

Why would he behave this way you might ask? Avoidant behaviors tend to be a defense mechanism for many people. The fear of confrontation with another person may override the knowledge that approaching situations differently could lead to better results. The emotional fear of conflict situations controls many people's ability to use rational approaches. I think my old boss didn't want to confront me because he was afraid of either damaging our relationship, or of having his feelings hurt by me.

When you first look at the Avoider your thoughts may go straight to cowardice, or lack of leadership. When you look a second time, a bit deeper, you can see that avoiding situations may not be as simple as an act of bravery. It may be a much deeper psychological belief that the Avoider is subject to in his or her life.

The Avoider may have a difficult time being in a leadership position since their behaviors to avoid conflict with other people cause internal conflicts to arise within themselves. Unknowingly avoiders cause pain within themselves while attempting to evade the pain caused by potential conflicts. Their behaviors directly result in the suppression of feelings about situations which may lead to internal turmoil, or passive aggressive tendencies. This is what happened with my former boss. He felt terrible inside for several months about a simple issue. His fear of confronting me caused him inexplicable amounts of stress for an extended period of time. If he had just come to me and talked about the situation it could've been resolved in 10 minutes.

Not all Avoiders have a deep-seated hesitation to engage in conflicts with others. Some simply avoid situations that they sense will cause negative feelings to keep the peace in the office. The motivation for this is simply to re-route potential negative feelings, and allow time for those involved to calm down. At times, this approach can be effective at defusing situations, but if it is used too often managers will become ineffective, and lose the respect of their employees.

Other managers are simply lazy. That's the cold hard truth. Some avoiders simply choose not to get involved in situations to save themselves from having to put forth the necessary effort to resolve the issue. These managers would do well to take another look at their motivation for doing what they do.

Tip: If you are an Avoider don't feel as though you're not a good manager. That was not my intention in this section. It is likely you are a good manager because you've been able to adapt to your personality. You definitely have the potential to learn how to overcome your avoidant behaviors and become more effective in your role as a manager. The first thing you might do is to identify yourself as an Avoider and own your behaviors. Next, ask yourself why you fear confrontation as much as you do? Once you have your answer ask yourself what is it about that answer that causes so much fear? Next, ask yourself what can you do to overcome this fear the next time? Then make a list of strategies to help you overcome these avoidance behaviors and try them. Start with something small and then move up to more arduous situations once you feel more comfortable. Taking these steps will help you own your fear, verbalize your fear, and overcome it.

The Accommodator: The next management style is characterized by accommodating behaviors. At first this sounds like a pleasant way to approach management. However, the Accommodator approaches management situations by changing him or herself to fit the needs of the other people involved. Again, seemingly this is a good way to approach management situations. If you take a deeper look you will see that the Accommodator puts the needs and wants of other people above him or herself to the point where he or she loses a sense of identity, or participation, in the situation. This management style seeks to avoid conflicts with others by simply taking themselves out of the equation. When the employee disagrees with something the Accommodator says and offers an alternative the Accommodator will quickly dismiss his or her own thoughts, feelings, or opinions and adopt the suggestions made by the employee.

Why would a manager be an Accommodator? Each manager has a unique personality. Some people prefer to put the needs, and wants, of others above themselves for a number of reasons. One reason may be that the person's personality is kind and generous. This type of manager wants to show his or her employees that he or she cares about them and listens to what they have to say. This motivation is pure in its intent but, leaves no room for the Accommodator to contribute his or her thoughts. Another motivation to be accommodating may be to avoid conflict. The accommodator may feel as though giving in to the requests of other people avoids the potential for conflict to arise. This relates back to the first management style in that avoidant behaviors dominate the decisions made by the manager.

Despite their motivation to accommodate others Accommodators lose their sense of self in situations, and may not be as effective as they are capable. This leads to a situation where employees feel as though they are equal to the manager in the decision-making process. This is a good concept to have among your employees however, there must be a clear definition between who is leading the team and who is on the team. The Accommodator lets go of too much control in favor of keeping people happy. This leads to a confusing situation in which employees may not understand where to go for guidance.

Tip: If you are an Accommodator you might look at what the motivation is behind your accommodating behaviors. Ultimately you desire to have everyone feel good about their work, and that they are a valuable part of the team. This is a fantastic sentiment to have in your office, and helps create very positive work environments. However, you need to be heard as well. If you feel as though you're not contributing as much as you would like, go through the steps associated with the Avoider to understand what is holding you back from providing your input. Once you've established what holds you back and why it holds you back you can overcome it by implementing these actions into your daily routine, and build a higher level of confidence.

The Competitor: On the other end of the spectrum from the Accommodator is the Competitor. The Competitor is just what it sounds like. The Competitor has a driving need to win conflicts, and to be right no matter who they are facing. This manager views conflict situations as a chance to face an opponent and win a small battle. At all costs the Competitor wants to be in the spotlight, and show everyone that he or she is the victor. This manager puts him or herself above everyone else, and views his or her opinions as being the only ones that matter. Everyone else to the Competitor is simply an opponent, and will be defeated if they get in the Competitor's way.

I once had a coworker who felt that everything was a competition. She and I were the same level, lower management, and worked together on a team. I, being the trusting soul that I am, originally thought that she and I would get along well, and do a lot of good work in the organization. How wrong I was! Soon after we began working together I noticed that the things she would say to me when we were working on a project were very different than those she would say to our supervisor. Then I started to notice that our supervisor was giving credit to my coworker for ideas that I had come up with and told her about. She had been taking my ideas and presenting them to our supervisor as if they were her own.

This was a lesson in how some people are competitors. My coworker didn't care that she was stealing my ideas. She only cared about herself and making herself look better in the eyes of the upper management. Because we were at the same level she viewed me as competition for future promotions, and gave herself a goal to win the battle. I was much more interested in working together to improve the program we were overseeing than competing against her for the chance of a nonexistent promotion. Unfortunately, we were unable to improve the program because of her ultra-competitive nature.

Having a competitive nature is much different than being the Competitor. A competitive nature motivates people to work hard and achieve goals, oftentimes in teams. The Competitor takes this notion to the extreme and either tramples everyone in their path, or only makes alliances with people they feel will help them win. Managers who are Competitors view their team as a machine which is to be used for winning every battle possible. These managers expect results from their employees, and don't care how they get them.

The Competitor as a manager may have good intentions in that they desire for their team to be the best possible to make the company stronger, and a better place to work. This intention may drive them to push their employees to achieve top results, but their methodology for achieving these results may cause strife amongst their employees. Employees don't like to be pushed harder than needed. They may feel as though their manager doesn't care about them and only cares about results. Unfortunately, for the Competitor this may be how things are. The ultra-competitive manager may not care about his or her employees, and may only desire to have results that are beneficial. This leads to a negative work environment and a lot of feelings of malcontent amongst employees.

Tip: If you are a Competitor take a look at your motivations for your level of competitiveness and decide whether lessening your intensity may be beneficial to your employees. Try to determine if there are other approaches you can take that may yield the positive results you're looking for. You might start by asking yourself, why do I have to win at all times? Once you have your answer ask yourself, what is it about this answer that truly motivates my actions? Once you narrow down the root cause for your behavior think about some strategies you can use to help alleviate some of the pressure you feel to act competitively. Try these out in your work environment and increase their frequency as you feel more comfortable.

The Intimidator: Some managers feel that the only way to get employees to do what they want is to make them feel threatened, or scared. These managers employ intimidation tactics in an effort to get employees to act. The Intimidator often yells at employees and speaks in an overly excited voice about situations to get his or her point across. The reason for being intimidating is to motivate employees to do their best work. The Intimidator may threaten to fire employees if they do not do their jobs to get them to complete their tasks. This manager typically doesn't understand any other method of leading their employees.

When I was a young man I had a boss who could always be heard coming. He was a nice guy, but you did not want to get him agitated. Even when he wasn't agitated he sounded as if he was every time he needed to explain something to any of us employees he shouted. Especially if someone was slacking off he would raise his voice and make everyone around feel uncomfortable. I was lucky enough to never get the worst of his yelling, but others weren't so lucky. He made sure to let everyone know that if he caught them doing something wrong he would fire them immediately. He kept us employees feeling as though he had our future in his hands which was very intimidating. It did not make for a good working environment.

Employees working under the Intimidator are not likely to feel good about themselves, or their workplace. These employees may work enough to keep themselves off the manager's radar, but will not be loyal employees. These employees will likely leave their companies the first chance they get. The Intimidator needs to learn about effective management styles and how he or she can implement more effective management practices.

Tip: If you are the Intimidator don't worry. Your motivations are likely of good intent. You just want your employees to do their jobs. Intimidating may be the only way you know how to get them moving, but there are other management styles that may be more effective. Take time to evaluate your management style and learn as much as you can about other styles. This will help you decide if implementing some changes will be the right fit for you.

The Compromiser: Many managers fall into one of the first four categories of management style, but after reading through these sections some of them may be able to re-evaluate their management style and embrace the style of the Compromiser. This management style is characterized by the idea of allowing for all thoughts, feelings, and opinions to be heard and given equal opportunity to put forth suggestions. The Compromiser values, and respects, the contributions of members of his or her team and takes their suggestions into consideration. This management style genuinely seeks out the thoughts, feelings, and opinions of employees, and attempts to create the most beneficial situation for everyone involved. The Compromiser understands that by gathering as many ideas as possible the more likely the team will be able to come up with a creative solution.

When I was earning my Master's degree I had several classmates with whom I worked on team projects.

Some of my classmates were not good team players, but some were. Those of us who worked well with each other teamed up often and learned how to function within the group. I generally took the role of project leader because I was good at assembling the various pieces of the project and making it look as if it had been created by one person. I remember one situation where my team and I had very differing opinions on what a project about psychological motivators should look like. I thought we should add some style to the presentation to make it more eye-catching. My teammates felt that we should make it more simple, and less of an eyesore. Each of us presented our side of what we thought the best course of action would be and took each other's opinions seriously. We ended up creating a project that met in the middle. It wasn't too flashy, and it wasn't boring. We respected each other's thoughts about the project and we created something far better than we could have on our own. We earned an A on that project.

    Through our efforts to compromise on these projects we helped each other receive high marks on our assignments. This was a valuable lesson in the rewards associated with compromising, and the benefits of combining ideas to create something better than we could have individually. The Compromiser understands that combining the efforts of the entire team and respecting the thoughts and ideas of each member creates an environment of openness and connectedness. This type of workplace is desirable to employees. Employees who are valued by their managers are motivated to provide their highest caliber work. Also, they take pride in knowing that they are respected, and are more likely to be loyal to their company.

Tip: The Compromiser gets things done in a manner that is respectful and encourages participation from everyone involved.

The Collaborator: The Compromiser and the Collaborator are essentially the same manager. I know the term collaborator makes you think of a person working with a foreign government in a spy movie. The Collaborator as a manager is one who utilizes the concepts of the Compromiser in situations involving multiple teams which may include different departments within an organization, as well as outside sources that will contribute to a project. The Collaborator emphasizes the importance of respecting the thoughts, feelings, and opinions of everyone involved, but on a larger scale than the Compromiser. This management style is based on mutual respect, and seeks to create the best solutions possible by taking into consideration all ideas from the various teams. The Collaborator helps to weed out ideas that won't work as well, and promote ideas that will be the most effective. The Collaborator understands that having a Compromiser on each team will help make certain that everyone is able to contribute.

Tip: This management style thrives on taking input from multiple sources and combining ideas to form the best possible solutions.

Which Style: Which style of management you choose to implement is up to you. One style is clearly more useful in the day-to-day operations of most managers, but each style has specific uses. At times it may be the right choice to avoid a situation. At another time it may be the right choice to accommodate the feelings of an employee. Being ultra-competitive will hardly ever be the proper choice in a management situation, but a healthy level of competition inspires employees to produce some high-quality work.

Compromising is the most useful management style for the vast majority of managers, unless you are managing multiple teams in which case the Collaborator would be more useful. Whether you're just starting out as a manager or have been at it for some time, working on your compromising skills will only benefit your career. The Compromiser is the manager who is successful day in and day out, month after month, year after year. By respecting the thoughts of everyone on your team you will be able to not only find creative solutions to problems, but also motivate your employees to constantly strive to produce their best quality work.

Tip: Be careful not to become the Accommodator when transitioning. Remember that you are the manager, and it is up to you to make the final decisions. Just be sure to provide opportunity for individuals to provide input.

Now that you've had a chance to learn about the different management styles take a few minutes to reflect on which manager you are. Ask yourself, am I who I want to be as a manager? Once you answer that question ask yourself what can I do to be a better manager? After you answer that question come up with a list of strategies you can implement to help yourself either become the manager you want to be by changing your management style, or by improving on the level of skill you already have.

In the next several chapters we will explore different aspects of management that are of the utmost importance to master to be an effective and efficient manager. We will take a look at the theory behind each of these concepts, as well as real-world examples of what these aspects of management actually look like. Through learning these principals and utilizing these systems you will be able to take away valuable information and develop management skills to help you succeed.

Chapter 2

Communication

How do I communicate effectively as a manager?

*"Persuasive speech, and more persuasive sighs,
Silence that spoke, and eloquence of eyes.."*

- **Homer**

Today I can pick up my phone and have a video chat with my in laws on the other side of the world. That wasn't possible a decade ago. Communication technology has grown by leaps and bounds in the past 20 years. At no point in human history has communication been more readily available to as many people as it is today.

Take for instance the first super computer developed at NASA. It ran at 40 MHz, and processed about 3,000,000 points of information per second. That was extremely fast in 1967. People couldn't believe that a machine could be capable of such speeds. Today, a little over 50 years later, the world's fastest super computer runs 3,300,000,000 times faster. That's 3.3 BILLION times faster than the first super computer![5] That's an almost unfathomable growth rate. Granted we don't use super computers in our everyday life, but we do use personal computers, cell phones, and video game systems.

In the 1980's the first commercially available cell phones came in heavy bags, were placed in cars, and could only send and receive calls.[6] Today I carry my cell phone in my pocket, receive text messages, receive e-mails, watch movies, and conduct research on the Internet all in the palm of my hand. I can be walking down the street, sitting on a bench, or even standing on the street in another country and still use my cell phone.

Why has so much attention been placed on developing our communication abilities? Why has so much money been invested in research and development of these technologies? Why is communication so important?

Communication is the lifeblood of all human interaction. Whether it is in your personal life or at work, communication is a necessary part of everyday life. We communicate our needs and wants to those we are close to. We communicate our fears and desires through our actions. We communicate how to get things done with our written and spoken words. We even communicate without thinking about it through our bodies sending messages to those around us. These are the reasons why so much emphasis has been placed on communication development.

3 Types of Communication

The way in which we communicate is largely dependent on the context of the situation. Using one form of communication over another may be a better choice depending on what's going on. No matter what kind of situation you are in there are three types of communication that you will use to get your point across. Written communication in the form of letters, e-mails, and text messages. Verbal communication in the form of speaking face-to-face, video conferencing, and speaking on the phone. And, nonverbal communication in the form of body language and gestures. These three types of communication convey the messages we send to other people. Learning to understand each of these types of communication will help you improve your communication skills, and become more effective at conveying your message.

Written Communication: One might think that with advancements in communication technology that written communication would be going the way of the dinosaur. However, written communication is just as important today as it was 50 years ago. Written communication may possibly be even more important today because writing skills have slowly diminished, and the demand for good writers has increased. Writing is needed for websites, articles, and e-books to name a few modern sources.

Writing efficiently can make all the difference in your life as a manager. If people are able to clearly understand what you are trying to say your life as a manager will become much easier. There are several key concepts to understand to help you improve your writing.

When I say improve your writing I'm talking about conveying your message in the most efficient manner possible. So, what is efficient writing? Efficient writing means that you are able to clearly, concisely, and professionally transfer a message using the least amount of written words necessary. You may be thinking that writing involves using as many words as possible to describe things so that the other person understands what you're talking about. Sometimes this is true, but is more likely used in non-business writing. Business writing needs to be as short as possible and as long as necessary. This means that in written communication you need to state all of the important facts, or instructions, while keeping the length of the letter to a minimum. Say what is necessary but, with as few words as possible. Take a look at *figure 1*.

> Dear Sir/Ma'am,
>
> I am writing to you today on behalf of XYZ Corp. Can see from our records that you showed interest in our products in the past. I would like to thank you for your interest and tell you about some of the most interesting things going on at XYZ Corp. We have been expanding our services department and reaching out to the community. We enjoy taking time to gain a better understanding of what our customers need through community programs. At times we even take field trips from work to go and explore the from parts of our city. This is fun for our employees and helps us to better our services.
>
> Speaking of our services we have reor-ganized some of our most popular packages to make the more efficient. Also, we've added several new features that are very exciting.

> If you get a chance take a look at our web-site at www.XYZ.com to browse through our service packages. If you see anything you like please call me at 1-888-888-888 so we can discuss connecting you with some of our new services packages.
>
>
> Thanks for your time,
>
> Jim Bob
>
> Service Sales

Figure 1 Bad Letter

    As you can see this letter is a bit long as it spills over on to a 2nd page. First, look at to whom the letter is addressed. Jim Bob hasn't even taken the time to find out to whom the letter should go to. There are a couple of grammar mistakes in the letter which looks unprofessional. Typos are inevitable, but taking a minute to reread will help ensure as few mistakes as possible. Also, if you look at the first paragraph Jim Bob goes into a lot of unnecessary detail about things going on in his company. The reader of this letter does not need to know that Jim Bob goes on field trips sometimes. The reader wants to know the point of the letter. People are busy. Taking up their time with needless details annoys some people which can affect your business.

Look again at *figure 1* the information Jim Bob is trying to convey is scattered and unclear. Does he want the recipient to call to discuss services? Does he want them just to go to the website? How is he trying to influence the reader to take some sort of action? When you're writing a letter such as this you need to make sure that the reader clearly understands what you are offering, and what you'd like them to do. Take a look at *figure 2*.

1/1/2121

Dear Ms. Smith,

     I was looking through our records and noticed that you purchased our Ultimate Services Package back in 2010. Since then we have made significant updates to the package which include several new bonus features. If you are interested in learning more about our new packages please contact me directly.

Have a great day,

Jim Bob

Service Sales

1-222-222-2222

jb@xyzcorp.com

Figure 2 Good Letter

In *figure 2* you can see that it is concise and to the point. Jane doesn't go into needless detail about things going on in her company. She simply says that Ms. Smith may be interested to learn about the new features of the service she is offering. Jane lets Ms. Smith know that there are many new features and bonuses associated with the updated package, but leaves the next action step in the hands of Ms. Smith. She calls Ms. Smith to action by asking to contact her directly. Also, you'll notice that her contact information is clearly stated in the signature underneath her name. Ms. Smith does not have to search through the letter to find Jane's e-mail address, phone number, or website address. It's presented clearly for easy access. This letter is clear in the message it is trying to convey. It is concise in that it uses only as many words as necessary. It is professional in that it addresses a specific person, is free from grammatical errors, and provides clear contact details.

The letter in *figure 2* may take a bit more effort to research the exact contact details for the person you are trying to reach within an organization, but will be infinitely more effective at selling services. Someone reading a letter wants to know the letter was written to him or her personally. They don't want a generic letter that's printed 100,000 times and sent randomly to people. Also, they want to see that the letter clearly states a point and does not waste their time with needless details. People will respond much more positively to your writing if you take these concepts into consideration.

This concept also applies to writing within your organization. You should not only focus on writing clearly, concisely, and professionally when interacting with outside sources. You should do the same when writing letters and e-mails within your own company. People in your place of business are busy as well. They want to read what you have to say, but they want to do it in as efficient a manner possible. They want to know what your point is and what they need to do. Taking the time to develop your writing skills will only benefit your career.

To improve your writing skill look at what you are writing. Ask yourself am I saying everything that needs to be said? It's important to remember that written communication needs to include all important details. Often when people are learning to be more concise in their writing they tend to leave out important details. Be sure to include all important details. Just eliminate the unnecessary information. Once you've determined that you have included all the necessary information seek out ways to say each of the points more concisely, clearly, and professionally.

For example,

"Tim, I need to get a copy of those reports that talk about at the meeting we had two days ago, on Wednesday, because I need to go over some of the information that was covered."

This seems like an okay sentence but, is there a way to make it more concise?

"Tim, please get me a copy of the reports from the meeting on Wednesday."

As you can see the sentence efficiently tells him what to do, "get me a copy of the reports". Also, the sentence tells Tim which reports specifically are needed. Tim knows that you want the reports from the meeting on Wednesday. The sentence is clear in that your message is said without misunderstanding. It is concise in that many words were eliminated from the original. The sentence is professional. It does not include unnecessary details about why the reports are needed simply that you want copies of the reports from the meeting on Wednesday. Tim does not necessarily need to know why you need something, he just needs to know it is needed.

Tip: It may seem cold to write this way, but to be efficient, time is extremely limited. You need to maximize the amount of time you spend completing tasks. Writing clearly, concisely, and professionally will help you to be much more efficient in how long it takes you to send e-mails and write letters.

Verbal Communication: What we say has more of an impact than most of us care to think about. Whoever said, "words don't hurt" was a liar. Words can hurt, but they can also bring happiness, understanding, and learning. The things that come out of our mouths can influence others positively or negatively.

Choosing the right words to say can make all the difference in the message you are trying to get across. The right words can inspire workers to put forth their best effort, and gain a sense of loyalty to their company. The wrong words can alienate employees, drive down their morale, and make them feel unappreciated. The right words can give employees hope in their future in your company. The wrong words can make them feel as though they are unwanted and useless to your organization. The right words can motivate employees to reach higher than they ever have before to achieve their dreams. The wrong words can crush the hopes of employees leaving them sad and unsatisfied. Words matter!

As a manager what you say to coworkers, employees, and business contacts plays a significant role in your work life. Having conversations, giving presentations, and negotiating sales with customers are all aspects of the daily life of a manager. The words you say greatly affect how these encounters play out. Finding the right words to clearly communicate your message can be difficult at times, but with practice you can learn how to be more efficient in the way you speak with others.

The most effective communicators in the world have spent a significant portion of their time studying the craft of speaking. There isn't one professional speaker today who would tell you that they have not invested a significant portion of their lives learning how to speak well. It takes time. It takes effort. It takes commitment. Learning how to communicate verbally is one of the most sought-after skills of managers today. Developing your speaking skills will benefit your entire career. Speaking can elevate you from an average employee to a great employee, or from an okay manager to a great manager.

A small town near where I grew up is well known for being the college home of a famous person. This person grew up working hard to pay his way through college. When he graduated he moved to Hollywood and became a well-known actor. After many years of acting he took a job with a large company where he traveled around the country speaking about products. After that he decided to start a career in politics. He went on to become the governor of

California, and eventually was elected as president of the United States.[7] This man was Ronald Reagan.

Reagan is known as the great communicator. Due to the years he spent studying acting he was able to develop the craft for speaking. Also, he was given ample opportunity to practice these skills when he worked as a professional speaker. Reagan did not wake up one day knowing how to be one of the world's greatest orators. He spent many years developing his craft, and learning how to ever improve upon his ability to speak in front of crowds. His verbal communication skills were directly related to his success in his career. Not only did they allow him to be elected into public offices, they also allowed him to communicate effectively with leaders from around the world. Speaking gave Ronald Reagan a chance to do something great with his life.

You and I may never run for president, but learning from the example of Ronald Reagan we can take away that speaking well can provide enormous opportunity in your career. Managers who are able to clearly verbalize what they want or need are much more effective at achieving results. Verbalizing what you need from employees in a clear manner eliminates confusion and misunderstandings.

Developing your skill as a speaker does not necessarily mean that you must speak in front of large crowds. It simply means that you've taken the time and effort to study how to be more effective at verbal communication. You can learn to speak well to one person and see positive results in your work life. If you become proficient at speaking to clients they will be more likely to buy from you. If you can become more proficient at speaking to your employees they will understand where you're coming from and what you'd like them to do. If you can become proficient at speaking to larger numbers of people you can communicate ideas. Ideas within companies can change the face of how an organization works. Verbal communication, done right, can be a game changer in your life as a manager.

How to improve your speaking abilities in 5 Steps

How do I improve my speaking abilities? How do I become more effective at verbal communication? What does it take to be a great speaker? These questions are all a bit subjective in that what is a great speaker to one person may be entirely different to another. However, whatever your goal is with improving verbal communication you will be able to develop your skill with a little hard work.

1.) **Write.** Write down all the areas in your work life in which you need to use verbal communication. These will include having conversations, giving presentations, and praising your employees.

2.) **Think.** Think about how you would approach each of these situations and what you might say. Is there a better way to say it? Can I improve the amount of time I spend in each of these areas if I reorganize how I am saying this?

3.) **Implement.** Apply the skills learned in written communication to your speaking. Ask yourself am I being clear in what I'm saying? Am I being concise? Is what I'm saying professional? This will help you eliminate a significant amount of unnecessary words. Also, remember to speak in a natural manner that reflects how you normally talk. Don't forget to slowdown. Rushing leads to misunderstandings.

4.) **Strategize.** Create a set of strategies you can use to assist you in utilizing these new speaking skills.

5.) **Practice.** Practicing speaking will help you grow in your ability as well as your confidence. The more you practice the better you will become, and the more comfortable you will feel with speaking in all types of situations.

Tip: Speaking may seem scary, but if you put forth the effort to learn as much about speaking as possible and practice your skills you will be able to rise above your fears and become comfortable in front of people.

Non-Verbal Communication. Now that we've discussed written and verbal communication let's take a look at what we say without thinking. Our bodies communicate more information than anyone really understands. Some researchers say that 70% of all communication is nonverbal.[8] Some say higher, some say lower. The point is the majority of what we communicate to other people is done without saying, or writing, a single word. Humans are constantly displaying gestures that reflect their inner thoughts and feelings. Most of these actions are completely unknown to each of us, and are only apparent when someone else points them out.

Take a look at someone around you and see if you can guess how they are feeling based on their body language. Look at the way they're holding their head. Is it up, down, or facing forward. What does this tell you about how they feel right now? Look at their body is it rigid, loose, or slouched. What does this say? Look at their hands. What are their hands doing? Are they rested and open, closed and tight, fidgeting, or buried in their pockets? What does this have two say about how they are feeling right now? Look at their legs and feet. What are their legs doing? Are they straight and relaxed, folded, jittery, or tapping their feet?
Now that you've spent some time thinking about the body language of other people let's look at an example.

You're sitting at your desk when you look up and notice that your coworker Tina is tapping her foot on the side of her desk. You noticed because you heard the sound and it distracted you from your work. When you look at Tina you see that she's also fidgeting with her hair and constantly looking back and forth between the clock and her computer screen.

What would you say Tina is feeling right now? If you said she's feeling anxious to leave work you're probably right. Tapping the foot, fidgeting, and constantly looking at the clock are clear indicators that she would rather be somewhere else right now.

Would you have guessed the same before we talked about observing her body language? Most likely you would have. Subconsciously we absorb information that is passed to us, and make judgments on the data we receive. Essentially our minds are computers that gather information, process that information, and formulate results. Every day we make judgments about how someone perceives us without thinking about why we feel that way. We feel that way because we subconsciously picked up the nonverbal communication that the other person was sending to us. Our brains processed the body language of another person, and decided that their behaviors indicated something either positive or negative about us. This all happened in the blink of an eye and without conscious thought.

Think about the last time you went on a date. You might not have been able to verbalize why you thought he or she liked you, but you knew that there was a connection. This type of subconscious processing of nonverbal cues is part of our daily lives.

As a manager what you say with your body is just as, if not more than, important as what you say with your written and spoken words. You can tell someone with your mouth that they're doing a great job, but your body may be telling an entirely different story. Your body may be telling them that you don't actually believe what you're saying, and that you're trying to get around the matter at hand. The Avoider is quite good at this. You may be genuine in what you're saying, but your body language may be working against you.

You might not be feeling very well one day so your body is sort of slouched, and your overall demeanor is unenthusiastic. When you go up to your employees to tell them they're doing a great job they may not believe you because you look and sound a little bit like Eeyore the donkey.[9] Your body is speaking much louder than your voice.

Paying attention to what your body is saying when you're speaking to other people will help you to be more effective in your communication. Making a conscious effort to display body language that conveys a message of trust, sincerity, and confidence will help you be more successful in your career from day one.

Think about some of the most influential people you know. What are the first things that come to mind when you think about them. Likely you would say that they are confident, well spoken, and trustworthy. Why do you say this? You say this because they display themselves that way. People in the public eye spend a great deal of time and money investing in their image. This has been true throughout the history of mankind. Politicians are especially well known for having coaches assist them with their body language. Take for instance Bill Clinton. He used to have a habit of holding out his index finger as if you were pointing at people in the crowd. People started to feel like he was singling them out, or that he was being condescending. Once his team figured out that people felt this way he had a coach help to think about his hand positions when he would speak publicly. After that he began holding up his fist with his thumb on top as if to hold his index finger from popping out.[10] This new gesture was perceived more positively by audiences. That one gesture made a world of difference in the thoughts and feelings people had about Bill Clinton.

What should my body look like when I'm speaking to someone? How do I improve my body language?

You too can learn to control your body language and display a more confident, vibrant you. You may need to ask someone you trust to help you with this, but by examining non-verbal communication you will be able to identify specific areas of your body that send out the wrong signals.

To get started either look in a mirror or have people you trust look at you when you are speaking about a work-related topic. Take notice of your head, shoulders, body, arms, hands, legs, and feet. Write down anything you notice about each one of these areas. Are there any specific areas that you notice something may be a little bit off? If so, think about that gesture and what it's sending to people around you.

Now that you've got a conscious understanding of your body language begin to think about how you can eliminate those gestures. Bill Clinton held his finger down with his thumb which was a physical means to control his body gesture. You may be able to eliminate certain behaviors simply because you're thinking about them, but you may need physical assistance to get creative, and to come up with a solution that works for you.

What you want to display:

Head – your head should be facing forward in a level position. Not tilted to the side, front, or back.

Shoulders – the shoulders should be facing the person, or people, you're talking to in the same direction as your head. Face forward.

Body – your torso should also be in line with your shoulders and head. If you want to display confidence hold your chest high but, not like a military officer.

Arms – your arms should be either at your side relaxed, or at a 90° angle resting on the podium.

Hands – you want your hands to be visible, not stuffed into your pockets. Your hands can be a powerful tool for gestures. To display openness show the palms of your hands when appropriate in a speech. Keep your hands relaxed and free.

Legs – your legs should be firmly underneath you. Don't slouch to one side or the other. Evenly distribute your weight on both of your legs.

Feet – keep your feet in a still position in front of you if you're sitting down, and in a straight line if you're standing up. Don't tap your feet as this is an indicator of nervousness.

Now that you understand the importance of your body language take the time to understand what you're saying with your body. Gaining a level of control over your body language will have noticeable effects on your ability to communicate effectively.

Tip: Taking time to understand what message you are displaying with your body will only serve to make you a better communicator. Put effort into developing your non-verbal communication and you will quickly see improvements in your communication ability.

Take Away

Written communication boils down to three concepts:

Clear – write as clearly as possible to get your message across.

Concise – write as concisely as you are able, but be sure to include all necessary information, and don't leave anything out.

Professional – write in a professional manner that conveys your position, and show courtesy to those reading what you've written.

Verbal communication will play a significant role in your work life. Investing in developing your skill as a speaker will only benefit your career for years to come.

Speak clearly. Speak in as natural a manner as you can and don't rush.

Speak concisely, but remember to fully explain necessary information.

Speak professionally. Use appropriate language and gestures when speaking.

Practice, practice, practice.

Body language accounts for the majority of human communication. Learning to understand and control your body language will help you develop your management skills.

Become conscious of what your body is saying.

Observe your head, shoulders, torso, arms, hands, legs, and feet.

Use physical means to stop behaviors if necessary.

Practice using effective body language to become more confident.

Chapter 3

Ethics and Credibility

How can I be an ethical manager?

"I have stepped out upon this platform that I may see you and that you may see me."

- ***Abraham Lincoln***

Ethics may seem like an uninteresting subject, but managing with ethical principles defines who you are as a leader. By developing a set of ethical principles by which to govern your managerial career you continue to be the person you want to be. At times we have all faced challenging situations in which we have had to decide to do what we knew was right, or to bend our ethical compass. An argument can be made that at times it is necessary to be flexible in your moral compass.

For example, if your child is starving do you steal a loaf of bread to feed him? That's a decision you have to make in that circumstance, but that is an extreme circumstance. In the world of business ethical decisions are often much easier to make than many people care to admit. It is often the case that ethical principles fall the way of the dodo when there are risks associated with doing the right thing. At other times ethical standards are stepped over in the pursuit of profit.

When I was working on my bachelor's degree I took a part-time job doing printer demonstrations in an electronics store. I didn't work for the electronics store, but I was contracted to stay in that store and do demonstrations of the printers. While I was there I had no direct supervision from my organization. The only manager there worked for the electronics store. One day I came into work and one of our printers was going on sale. I thought it would be a good day to sell as this was a very nice printer, and people would be excited to get a good deal. Soon after I started I sold one of the printers and sent the customer on their way. After that customer left the store manager came up to me and told me not to sell any more of that printer. I asked him why, and he stated that the markup on other printers was higher, so he wanted to sell them first. I said that my job is simply to demonstrate my company's printers to customers, and that if they asked me about that printer I would give it to them. I felt that was the right thing to do. He looked at me strangely and walked away. A few minutes later a worker from the store came up and took the printers from the shelf and carted them to another aisle. I thought this was strange, so I went to find where the worker put the new printers. I found them and returned to my post. Not long after that another customer came in and asked about the printer that was on sale. The electronics store worker told the customer that they were sold out and began to show them the printer that wasn't on sale.

    At this juncture I had to make a choice. Do I go along with what the manager told me, or do I stand on my ethical principles and sell the printer to the customer. I decided that it was wrong to lie to customers and tell them that they were sold out when we clearly had stock. The worker went to look for something else. I approached the customer and told them that I knew of a printer in the back. He was excited, so I went to grab a printer for him and put it in his cart. The worker returned and saw what I had done. He quickly ran off to report to his manager.

    By the time the worker and manager came back I had given the customer ink cartridges and the cable he needed to attach the printer to his computer. As he was walking away the worker stopped the customer asked if he would rather have a different brand cable. I gave him the most affordable cable because that's what he needed. The customer told the worker that he was set and didn't want to change anything that he had. As he was walking away another worker approached him and started talking to him about an extended warranty. While this was going on the first worker took the cable out of the man's cart and replaced it with the store brand cable which cost $2 more than the one I gave him.

    I was shocked to see this happen. As I was about to say something to the man the manager stepped in, impolitely let me know that this was his store, and that I had to do what he told me. I simply told him that he was not my boss, and that I was not going to do anything unethical or illegal. He became enraged and started shouting in the middle of the store. I simply turned around and went back to my work.

    I learned then that ethics was an important aspect of business and that standing on my moral compass was more important to me than making an extra $2.

    The store manager was so wrapped up in making a profit that he lost sight of any ethical standards. This not only affected the way in which he worked, but also trickled down to his employees. The lesson his employees were learning from him was that money was much more important than customers or morals. Those were lessons that his employees likely still remember today. If he had been an ethical manager he could have taught his employees the value of ethics and given them the skills they could apply to their careers for the rest of their lives.

Why do ethics matter?

Ethics matter because they are a representation of who you are as an individual and as a worker. You often hear the phrase, "It's not personal, it's just business." In my experience this has never been the actual case. People don't buy from a company; they buy from other people. The sales person is simply a man or woman who wants to provide a product to a consumer. A consumer is simply a person who wants to buy a product. When the consumer speaks to a salesperson they are speaking to a human being, not a machine. This, by definition, is personal. Salespeople must make a connection with the consumer if they want to make a sale.

If you have a strong set of ethical principles your sincerity will be shown to consumers. Sincere salespeople who want to provide a consumer with the product they need, rather than just sell them as much as possible, will be much more effective in the long run, and more successful in their career.

Conducting business with ethics helps you build a reputation as being an honest and trustworthy person. Would you rather go to a person who has a reputation for being honest, or to the person who has a reputation for selling you things you don't need? Obviously, you'd like to go to the person who has a reputation for being honest.

Who wants to go to someone who's just out to take their money rather than someone who will genuinely care about helping them get what they need? I don't think anyone would say they would rather go to the dishonest person, unless they are doing something illegal, in which case this section doesn't apply. If you are acting legally though, you'll want to do business with someone who has a reputation for being trustworthy.

Once you've established a reputation as being honest and trustworthy your ethics have assisted you in creating a long-lasting career path. People often think that giving in to ethical choices here or there will not hurt them. But, a reputation takes years to earn, and only seconds to destroy.

Another way that implementing a strong ethical guideline into your work life will help your career is by helping to establish your credibility. Credibility is a form of reputation in which people know you as a person who can get things done in a specific field. In your office you may be known as the manager who is great at motivating employees. This means that you have credibility amongst your coworkers because you reliably achieve success when you're called upon.

This is mostly achieved by doing what you say you will do, and doing it right. If you tell people you will do something, do it. If you tell people you will get something done, but don't, you are only wasting their time, and possibly their money. Wasting people's time is a surefire way of earning a bad reputation. If you do what you say you will people will respect the fact that you get things done and your credibility will grow. If you don't do what you say you will people will quickly let others know not to count on you.

   A friend of mine and his wife were buying a house. After the long wait for paperwork the bank said that they would have the documents ready to sign on Friday. Friday came around, my friend took the day off work, and the person working on the mortgage papers called to tell them that the papers weren't ready yet. This would've been useful information the day before as my friend took the day off work without pay. But, what could they do? The person working on the mortgage papers promised them that Monday afternoon the papers would be ready and that they could come in and sign them. She said that the people she sent the papers to were taking a long time, and that she was trying to rush them along.

   Monday came around, my friend took the day off again, and he and his wife waited for the bank to call. At about 5 minutes till closing time the bank worker called and said that the papers still weren't ready, but promised that they would be ready tomorrow. This happened for the next four days in a row. My friend was off work the entire week without pay because the bank worker didn't turn in the documents until the Thursday before.

The bank worker never explained this to my friend and his wife, they found out through their realtor. The bank worker kept telling them that it was the fault of the people she sent the papers to, but in reality, it was her fault for not turning the papers in sooner. My friend lost an entire week's pay because the bank worker did not conduct business with them ethically.

When you have a family to take care of a week's pay is a significant hit to your budget. As a direct result of the unethical practices of this bank worker my friend not only lost income for his family, but also lost time from his job. The implications of this worker's lack of ethics had real world effects on my friend's family. If she had been honest from the beginning my friend could've worked the entire week, and just signed the papers when they were ready. She decided to manipulate them, and disregard the negative consequences her unethical actions had on my friend's family.

How to improve work ethics in 4 steps.

1.) Ask: Ask yourself whether any parts of your work make you uncomfortable? Then ask yourself why you are uncomfortable with these parts of your work life?

2.) Develop: Develop a set of personal ethical standards that you can apply to your work. You can create a list based on your personal beliefs according to religion, world views, and life choices.

3.) Compare: Look at your list and compare it to your company's formal policies, as well as the unwritten rules at your workplace. Often workplaces have a set of unwritten guidelines that workers are expected to follow. Compare your personal ethical standards and determine if they align.

4.) Implement: If they do align you are good to go. Just think about ethical choices when difficult situations arise. If they do not align, you may have to rethink your career path, or attempt to create changes in your workplace.

Take Away:

Choosing to conduct your work life by a set of ethical standards will help you establish a reputation for being honest, trustworthy, and credible.

Ethics provides a set of guidelines to help you make the right choices.

Ethics helps you become a trusted provider, which will help you have a successful career.

Making ethical choices at work will help you to feel good about yourself in all aspects of your life.

Ethical choices are not only good for you personally, but are good for the people you are helping.

Chapter 4

Interviewing

How do I interview people, and know who to hire?

"Do not hire a man who does your work for money, but him who does it for the love of it."

- ***Henry David Thoreau***

When you set out to conduct interviews it generally means one of two things. Either a position has opened up because your current employee moved to another location, or your business is growing and you need to hire more people. Whatever the reason for seeking out a new employee, approaching the interview process with a plan in mind is a wise choice. Many managers dread the interview process as it takes time, effort, and can be a bit drawn out. As Katherine Hepburn is believed to have said, "Death will be a great relief. No more interviews." She was talking about interviews with reporters, but I think the sentiment applies to a lot of managers. Some managers enjoy the process because they like meeting new people, but many managers find it uncomfortable to ask strangers personal questions about their lives. Whether you enjoy the interview process or not taking time to plan out a strategy for how to conduct interviews will allow you to be much more efficient at the process.

Going into the hiring process with a specific plan in mind of how you accomplish each task provides you with a set of guidelines to rely on. This will help you make the most out of every aspect of interviewing, and help you choose who to hire. Deciding upon a strategy and creating a structure for interviews will be well worth your time investment.

Interviewing Strategies

Interviewing strategy depends on the organization, for which department you are hiring, and the type of employee for which you are searching. To help you determine what strategy will best suit your individual hiring needs we will explore four strategies. These strategies focus on different areas of interest when trying to decide if the interviewee will be a good fit for your company.

Fact-Based Interview Strategy. This strategy focuses on obtaining factual information from candidates based on their knowledge of specific areas of business. The aim with fact-based interview strategy is to ensure that the person you are hiring has the real-world knowledge necessary to be successful in the role you are trying to fill. This strategy focuses less on personality and more on knowledge.

Why choose this strategy? This strategy is most useful when trying to find an individual who will work in a technical arena, and who may not have to participate much as a team member. Because this person would not be interacting often with other team members, their personality is less important to the job than his or her knowledge.

How do you prepare for this strategy? To prepare for this strategy you need to establish a comprehensive set of guidelines for what the job entails. Then, create a series of questions that will identify whether the candidate possesses the knowledge necessary to be successful in this role.

Tip: Create a list of keywords that are important to the job aspects you are looking for and listen for them when the candidate is speaking.

Technical-Based Interview Strategy. To utilize a technical-based strategy the focus will be on whether the candidate has the technical skills necessary to be successful in the job. Many jobs require a level of skill that cannot be overlooked. At times, candidates may overestimate their abilities on certain aspects of technical skills. This is not to say they're bad people just that their personal assessment of their own skills may be a little bit off target.

Why choose this strategy? This strategy helps to confirm that candidates possess the necessary skills for the job. Because technical knowledge is necessary for the position you must know that a candidate is capable of successfully completing all job tasks.

How do you prepare for this strategy? Create a comprehensive list of all technical skills necessary to be successful in this job. Then, design a practical test that you will administer to the candidates in the interview process. This could be a computer skills tests, salesmanship test, assembly test, etc. Once they complete the test, assess whether they have the necessary skills for the job.

Tip: Make sure that the test covers all the major aspects of the technical skills you will need so that you do not waste the candidate's time, or yours.

Situation Based Interview Strategy The situation based strategy emphasizes scenarios that candidates will find themselves in if they are hired. This strategy revolves around trying to understand if a candidate will be successful in the situations that the job requires. Each job is unique and has a different setting. Candidates must be able to demonstrate that they will be able to successfully complete tasks. For instance, if you are hiring someone to be a factory worker you need to validate that he or she will be comfortable in the factory environment.

Why choose this strategy? This strategy helps determine whether a particular candidate will be comfortable in the setting you'll provide for the job. Some people thrive in an office environment, some thrive in working outdoors, and some love the ever-changing environment of traveling for work. Finding a person whose personality fits the situational requirements of your position may make all the difference in their ability to succeed. Hiring someone who has never traveled outside their home state to be an international representative may not be the right fit. The candidate may seem enthusiastic about getting to travel for work, but may not understand the realities of international travel. Determining whether a candidate is the right fit for your working conditions will help you hire the best person for the job.

How do you prepare for this strategy? Create a description of the working environment in which the candidate will be placed. Identify any specific scenarios that may be a challenge for candidates, but are necessary for completing the job tasks you require. Create a list of scenarios that the candidate will find him or herself in, and create questions that will help you conclude if the candidate will be successful in these situations.

For example, if you are looking to hire a person as a personal assistant you could ask," What are your ideal working conditions?" Follow up with questions that lead to a more in depth analysis of the candidate's suitability for this position by asking questions such as, "How do you feel in an office setting?" Listening to the answers the candidate provides will allow you to gain an understanding of how he or she feels about your work setting.

Tip: Be creative with questions based on scenarios so that you can elicit multiple responses. Look for consistency in the answers to decide whether the candidate will be the right fit for the position.

Confrontation-Based Interview Strategy. This strategy may be the most difficult for managers to implement because it requires a level of comfort with confrontation. Many jobs require employees to handle a significant amount of stress while remaining calm and professional. If the position you're hiring for requires candidates to be in situations that will potentially put them in stressful situations you need to know before you hire them that they are able to successfully navigate these scenarios. Confronting candidates in the interview process will allow you to see how they react to stressful situations, and make assessments on whether they will be successful in the position or not. Many of the largest consulting firms in the United States utilize this approach to weed out potential candidates who are unable to thrive under pressure.

Why choose this strategy? The position you are hiring for may not be quite as stressful as that of the consultant, but may have its own unique set of stressful situations. No matter what the circumstances are for the position for which you're hiring, you need to understand if a candidate will be able to handle the pressure that comes along with the job. Utilizing the confrontational strategy will help you determine that candidates are able to remain calm under pressure.

How do you prepare for this strategy? Create a list of stressful situations that the candidate will find him or herself in if they are hired. Think about what level of stress will be required, and create a set of questions that will allow you to imitate this level of stress in the interview.

For example, some large companies will randomly ask questions such as, "How many cubic inches are in this room?" This question catches candidates off guard because they have no way of telling the exact dimensions of a room without a measuring tape. The purpose of this kind of question is to test if they remain calm, and attempt to provide a rational answer to your question. You can also approach this by mounting an "attack" on the candidate's resume by asking stressful questions about gaps in the work experience. Listen to the answers that are provided, and assess the candidate's ability to perform under pressure.

Tip: Be creative with the questions you ask to elicit responses. Be careful not to overdo the amount of stress you place on candidates. Keep it at the same level as the job will require.

How to choose a strategy.

Each of these strategies is unique in its focus, and will help you approach the interview process with a plan in mind. Utilizing one of these strategies will help you make decisions about selecting candidates. If you find that using one of the strategies does not cover all the aspects of the job, create your own strategy by combining certain aspects of these four strategies. Mix and match the aspects you require to create a strategy that best suits the needs of your company, as well as your personal preferences.

For example, you may utilize the situation-based strategy as the primary approach, but you may want to mix in some confrontational questions. Develop your strategy to fit your needs. The more thought and effort you put into creating a strategy, the more likely you will be at efficiently finding the right person for the job.

Tip: You may also find it useful to have two or more interviews for a candidate. The first interview may utilize the situation-based strategy. The second interview may focus on the confrontation based strategy. Develop your interview process to best fit your individual needs.

Interviewing skills

Companies often spend a great deal of time and money on improving their interviewing techniques. Hiring the right people for jobs is the most important aspect of the success of a company. A company cannot function without people. Employees are the heart and soul of any organization. Hiring the right people for the jobs you have will make all the difference in your company's ability to be successful.

Putting forth the effort to create an interview strategy and structure will help you become as efficient and effective as possible at hiring the right personnel. At times, a less structured process may be more beneficial, but for the majority of interviewing situations the better prepared you are the more likely you will be at finding the best person for the job.

Now that you've got a strategy and structure for the interview process there are two main skills that will help you be effective at determining the suitability of candidates.

Active listening. I am sure you've heard many times that listening is an important skill in the workplace. This is never more apparent than in the interviewing process. As a manager you may be required to conduct interviews on a seemingly unending basis. When so many interviews are conducted some managers blend applicants together and become disinterested in what is being said. It may be challenging to avoid this behavior, but it may also be crucial to your success in finding the right applicant. Before each interview make yourself ready to listen to what the candidate is going to say. Here are some steps you can take to help you use active listening skills.

Make as much eye contact as you can with an applicant, without making him or her feel uncomfortable.

Clarify statements made by applicants by repeating what they've said in a manner which lets them know that you are listening. For example," So, you've been to China? How was that experience?" or," That's great that you've participated in a lot of team projects because, we are very team oriented here."

If you feel yourself starting to tune out lean a bit forward toward the candidate. This shows them that you are interested in what they're saying, and helps you to engage in the conversation.

Don't interrupt an applicant while he or she is making a statement. Wait for them to finish and then ask them follow-up questions regarding what they said.

Tip: The more eye contact you make the better. It helps the applicant to feel as though you are genuinely acknowledging what they have to say. This helps them to be more comfortable with the entire interview process.

Body language

Body language in an interview can be quite telling of a candidate's personality traits. As we explored in *Chapter 2* body language is extremely important in the message we are sending to other people. As an interviewer you want to display your body language in a non-threatening manner to help candidates feel more comfortable with the meeting. Refer to *Chapter 2* for tips on controlling your body language.

As for the candidate, look at his or her body language and what it tells you about how he or she is feeling. Look at the candidate's head, shoulders, torso, arms, hands, legs, and feet (if you can see them). Is there anything noticeable about the behaviors they are displaying with their body?

Are they nervous? – Foot tapping, handshaking, jittery movements.

Are they hiding something? – Looking away from you, refusing to make eye contact, becoming defensive when you ask a question.

Are they defensive? – Rigid legs and body, arms crossed over their chest, unwilling to fully answer questions.

Are they relaxed? – Body loose, but not slouching, hands open or lightly clasped, facing you with their entire body and head, appropriate hand gestures.

Are they too relaxed? – Slouching, crossed legs, arrogant hand and body gestures.

Looking at candidates' body language and making an assessment on how they feel at this time will help you to draw some conclusions about their personalities. Follow your gut when it comes to the impressions you're picking up, but be careful not to over judge the person's body language as the interview process is stressful. Some people may just be nervous and are displaying body language that you are perceiving as being arrogant, disinterested, or unenthusiastic. Take body language into consideration as a piece of the entire package that the candidate is offering to your company during the interview process.

Tip: Watch for cultural differences in body language. Some cultures express body language differently than others. Be open to learning about cultural differences and how they show up in body language.

How to conduct interviews in 4 Phases.
Now that you've developed a strategy for the interview process you can design a structure to follow while meeting with candidates. The basic structure for an interview is as follows:

1.) Introduction phase
2.) Q&A phase
3.) Investigation phase
4.) Wrap up phase

1.) **Introduction phase:** This is the first encounter you have with the candidate in person. When they come into the interview room greet them by shaking their hand and welcoming them to the interview. In this phase it is important to help the candidate feel comfortable and relaxed. Interviews can be very stressful for people. Some people may be fantastic at their job, but have a hard time with the pressure of interviews. To help alleviate the stress begin by asking some personal questions of a friendly nature such as," Did you find the building okay?" After they answer that question ask them something else such as, "Are you originally from this area?" Asking these types of questions allows candidates to alleviate some of their stress by focusing on something unrelated to making a good impression on a potential new boss. This allows them to ease into the interview process and relax before you begin the Q&A phase.

Tip: Don't spend a great deal of time on this, but make sure that the candidate is comfortable and a bit more relaxed. This will help ease the tension for the candidate as well as for you.

2.) Q&A phase: During this phase of the interview process you will be asking the candidate questions to determine if they will be a good fit for your company. You can do this by studying their resume and asking them questions about the experiences they've had, their education, and any gaps in information you notice on the resume. Keep the Q&A phase structured, but allow for a bit of flexibility as well. This will help keep the interview rolling in a smooth fashion.

Tip: Keep the Q&A phase as light as possible unless you are utilizing the confrontation based strategy. Ask candidates to elaborate on their experiences. For example, if they indicate on their resume that they have traveled to another country ask them to describe their experience. Listen for the enthusiasm they show about their experience to get a feel for their personality.

> **3.) Investigation phase:** Design your questions based on the strategy you have decided upon, and have a prepared list of questions to ask the candidate before they arrive at the interview. Use your list to cover the information necessary to determine if they will be a good fit, but be flexible so that you can add in questions you notice about answers the candidates provide. Follow-up questions may lead to a significant amount of information that you would not have otherwise learned. Depending on the strategy you are utilizing, ask questions based on specific situations, facts, and technical knowledge necessary for the job. Asking a series of investigative questions will help you conclude if they not only have the necessary skills, but also the personality traits to best fit your organization.

Tip: When designing your interview use questions that are open ended and cannot be answered with a yes or no response. This will lead to much more elaborate responses from candidates, and allow you to get a more genuine picture of their skills, knowledge, and personalities.

> **4.) Wrap up phase:** After you've gotten all the information you need from a candidate open the floor to the candidate to ask questions he or she may have about the job. Encourage the candidate to ask as many questions as they need to feel comfortable even if you have already decided that they will not be a good fit for your company. The last thing you want to do is make a candidate feel bad about the interview. Also, if you are feeling like the candidate may be a good fit allowing them to ask questions may help support your instinct to hire this person. This allows the candidate to gain a more comprehensive picture of what will be required of him or her, as well as to gain further knowledge about what the job will entail. Once all the questions are finished stand up, shake the candidate's hand, and thank him or her for coming to the interview. Standing up shows the candidate that the interview is over and that they are free to go.

Tip: Some candidates will need a bit of encouragement to ask questions at the end of an interview. It may not be that they didn't have questions in mind, it may just be that they have forgotten them under the pressure of the interview. Ask the candidates questions such as," Do you have any questions about the job requirements?" Or, "Did I fully explain the working conditions that the job requires?" Sometimes asking these types of questions will help candidates to remember questions they thought of earlier.

Take away:

Interviewing is the front line for filling your company with employees who will provide high-quality service and make your business a success. The greater effort you put into planning a strategy and structure for your interviewing process the more efficient you will become at finding the right employees for your organization.

Fact based interview strategy – emphasizes employee knowledge over personality.

Technical based interview strategy – emphasizes the skills necessary for the job by utilizing job-related tests.

Situation based interview strategy – emphasizes the importance of determining if a candidate will be able to thrive in the working conditions you are providing.

Confrontation based interview strategy – emphasizes a confrontational nature in the interview to determine how well the candidate handles stressful situations.

Chapter 5

Teams

How do I manage effective teams?

Coming together is a beginning.

Keeping together is progress.

Working together is success.

-attributed to **Henry Ford**

Teams are made up of individuals who each bring unique skills and personality characteristics to the table. Teams can be made up of individuals from various backgrounds and from different departments. Depending on the needs of the team its members should be carefully selected to fill specific roles that will contribute to success. Building strong teams will allow you to maximize the output of your company, or department, and achieve more goals than you would by only managing talented individuals.

Michael Jordan is believed to have said, "Talent wins games but, teamwork and intelligence win championships." He understood the principle that teamwork allows people to do far more than they could on their own.

Teams within a company can help achieve business goals by combining efforts of individuals into a collaborative system of pooling skills, knowledge, and ideas. From this collaboration many new ideas can be formed, and creative solutions can be found. Managing teams is a skill that requires knowledge of your employees, their talents, and their personalities. It is the manager's responsibility to determine who will be the most effective at working together, and why each member is a valuable addition to the team.

What are teams?

Teams can be found throughout most walks of life. If you look around, you'll see teams almost everywhere. Athletic teams such as those in football, musical teams such as your favorite band, academic teams such as chess clubs, etc. It's easy to find teams wherever you look, especially in companies.

Even if a company does not have formal teams set up they have structures that create team environments such as the accounting department, the marketing department, or the sales department. Though these individuals may be working on their own they are still part of a team who is focused on the same goals. They may not work in a collaborative effort, but they are still contributing to the success of the team in one way or another.

To simplify the meaning of a team in a business environment it can be defined as a group of individuals who pursue one goal, have respect amongst each other, and share talents and resources to achieve results.[13] These three variables encompass what it means to be on a team.

First, the members must pursue one goal. The goal is to work together to achieve success in areas that an individual would either be unable to, or would take a far greater amount of time to accomplish. Managers need to assemble teams according to the ultimate goals of a project. Each team member you select needs to understand that his or her purpose is to contribute to the success of the team without individual recognition. That's not to say that you cannot compliment employees who are doing a great job within a team, but that will be covered in *Chapter 8*. The point is that each team member is focused on pursuing the same goal and understands how his or her contribution helps the team become successful.

Second, team members need to be ready and willing to share their talents, skills, and knowledge with the team to provide the highest quality work for which they are capable. Team members need to understand that holding back from full participation in the hopes to achieve individual success will only hurt the ability of teams to be productive. Managers need to make certain that team members are putting forth their best efforts to contribute their full talent to the success of the team. Managers must choose teammates who understand this principle, and who are ready and willing to join forces with other coworkers in the pursuit of one goal.

Third, team members must have respect for each other if they want to have any hope of success. If team members have no respect for each other they will not be able to work together and contribute to their full capacity. At times, one team member may feel they are not being recognized for their efforts and will either not contribute to the team, or ask to be removed. Managers carry the responsibility of ensuring that respect is apparent in all teamwork. If you come across situations where teams are not respecting each other you will be required to resolve the conflict. Conflict resolution is explored in *Chapter 9*. Teams that are respectful of each other will be able to thrive and achieve great success.

Types of team members

Team members are selected from your employees. As you get to know your employees you begin to understand their personalities, strengths, and weaknesses. As you do so you are likely to classify them into one of six categories.

The leader: Certain personality types convey leadership qualities better than others. As you learn the personalities of your employees you will see people within the office who have a natural tendency to take on leadership responsibilities. You can tell if a person is a natural leader by the reaction other employees have toward him or her. If other employees constantly ask this person for help, opinions, and suggestions they are likely viewed as a trusted source of information outside of management. This can be a good indicator of someone who will be successful at leading a team as he or she has already established leadership qualities amongst coworkers.

The implementer: This type of team member demonstrates the qualities of attention to detail, a strong work ethic, and a desire to produce top quality work. This person strives to make certain that anything with his or her name on it is the best work possible. He or she may be a bit of a perfectionist, but plays a key role in keeping teams running smoothly. The implementer ensures that each aspect of the project is completed correctly and compiled in the proper manner. This helps the team move to other aspects of the project while the implementer takes care of the details.

The thinker: Some employees are very good at coming up with ideas about how to solve problems. These people provide a valuable service to teams in that they are often inspired to come up with new ideas by listening to what others have to say. At times the thinker comes up with great ideas, but may not be able to come up with solutions to implement his or her suggestions.

The contributor: This person is usually quiet and very knowledgeable. The contributor is good at taking ideas from the thinker and creating ways to bring those ideas to life. This person plays a key role in the practical application of completing a project. He or she may not contribute as many new ideas, but without him or her many ideas would never come to life.

The builder: This team member is good at taking several pieces of information and determining how it fits together. The builder plays a key role in teams by taking various pieces and combining them into one project. The builder is good at solving problems, and allows for other team members to work on new pieces of a project while he or she compiles the other parts.

The inquisitor: You can always spot the inquisitor by his or her natural tendency to question ideas, or challenge suggestions made by coworkers. The inquisitor is not necessarily against any of the ideas or suggestions. He or she simply needs to have more information to feel comfortable with how, and if, an idea will work. This team member plays a pivotal role in ensuring that ideas proposed by other team members will be the most beneficial to the project. He or she is good at asking questions that force details to emerge that may be important to the project.

The outsider: The outsider is not one of your employees. This person is usually a consultant brought in to help complete a project. Consultants can be utilized to fill in gaps in teams where you do not have one of the six types of team members mentioned earlier. Consultants should be included in the team as if they were a regular member to increase the chance of success.

Tip: Some team members will be able to fill two roles. Team leaders are often good at being builders as well. Sometimes it is to your vantage to allow team members to fill two roles, but if possible try to have individuals fill each position on the team.

How to pick teams in 6 steps

To choose a team, managers need to fully understand the project they will be working on and, whether the team will be a temporary force, or a permanent placement. The difference between a temporary team and a permanent team can make a large difference in the success of grouping workers together. Some workers can work well with each other for short periods of time, but would not be suited on permanent teams together. As a manager, you will have to match the personalities of your employees to complement each team you create.

1.) **Decide:** You must decide if the team will be led by you, or as a self-managed team. If you will be leading a team you already have one of the six members. If you are not leading the team yourself, you'll need to choose a team leader from your employees.

2.) **Create:** Create a description of the project, or permanent structure, for which you need a team and make a list of the skills, knowledge, and personality traits necessary.

3.) **List:** Make a list of your employees by classifying them into one of the six categories above: the leader, the implementer, the thinker, the contributor, the builder, and the inquisitor.

4.) **Explore:** Look at the personality traits of your employees and determine if they will be able to work together well on a team. Take note of any office conflicts that have arisen in the past, and try to avoid putting coworkers together who have personality clashes.

5.) Select: From the employees you have who meet the requirements select members to fill each of the roles.

6.) Inform: Notify employees that you would like them to join a team, let them know why they have been chosen, and what their role will be on the team.

Once you've selected your team members bring them together and discuss how you would like the team to function, and the importance of focusing on the same goal, sharing their knowledge, and being respectful of one another. This will help to confirm that you have chosen a team that will work well together to achieve success.

Tip: You will be able to know that you have a team that works well together if you hear team members saying words such as, "we", and "us" as opposed to, "I", and "me" around the office.

Take away:

Picking successful teams is an important aspect of the manager's responsibility. When choosing teams be sure to put forth the effort to understand the strengths, weaknesses, and personality characteristics of each of your employees. This will allow you to assign each employee to one of the six roles of a team member.

The leader – Provides guidance to teams and inspiration to achieve results.

The implementer – Makes sure projects run smoothly by paying attention to details.

The thinker – Comes up with great ideas and is inspired by suggestions made by team members.

The contributor – Has the ability to contribute knowledge and solutions to implement ideas.

The builder – Puts all the pieces of a project together to make it cohesive.

The inquisitor – Challenges ideas to make sure that they will be the best choice for the project.

Chapter 6
Employee motivation
How do I motivate my employees?

Management is nothing more than motivating other people.

— attributed to **Lee Iacocca**

Employee motivation is a crucial aspect of daily business. Motivated employees tend to work hard and enjoy their jobs. Unmotivated employees tend to hold negative feelings about their jobs and dread going to work. A motivated workforce is one that produces high quality results and has positive attitudes about their company.

A manager's goal should always be to motivate that his or her employees. To do so managers need to understand how employees find motivation. Employees are motivated by three main factors: compensation, working conditions, and supervision, which is you.

Before we get into motivational factors let's look at how employees view motivation. How employees view motivational aspects of the job is dependent on their personal beliefs about what they deserve. These beliefs can be classified into 1 or 2 systems. To explain these belief systems two researchers named Victor Vroom and John Stacy Adams came up with theories. Let's explore Vroom's Expectancy Theory and Adams' Equity Theory.

Vroom's Expectancy Theory

Expectancy theory revolves around the idea that workers believe that the harder they work the greater the rewards they will receive.[14] Rewards come in the form of compensation for their work (pay, benefits, time off, etc.), and recognition from supervisors. Employees believe that the more effort they put into their work the more they will be recognized and rewarded. The focus of expectancy theory is on the individual worker and what he or she receives for putting forth effort.

Employees expect to receive fair compensation for their effort. What's fair? Each individual employee creates a set of guidelines that he or she judges the fairness of what the company is providing to reimburse his or her efforts. Some employees place a greater value on the amount of pay they will receive for their work, while others are more interested in the benefits provided. For some employees it may be more crucial to have quality health benefits for their families than to have a higher paycheck, or vice versa. A man or woman with a family will likely place greater emphasis on quality health benefits than a younger person who does not yet have children. The mix of combining rewards for compensation is completely dependent on the individual.

Employees also expect to be recognized by their supervisors for their efforts. Employees believe that the harder they work the greater rewards they will receive. Recognition from supervisors for a job well done is a significant reward to most employees. People like to be recognized for their hard work and appreciated for what they contribute to the company. Providing public and private recognition to employees helps to motivate them to continue to put forth enough effort to produce good enough work to be recognized. Sometimes a simple pat on the back and a "good job" is a powerful tool for keeping employees motivated.

For a company to be successful employees must believe that the rewards they receive for their work are valuable enough to put forth their best efforts. If they do not believe that a company is appreciating their labors they will not be motivated to give any effort beyond what they feel the company deserves. This individual mindset must be taken into consideration when determining how to reward your employees.

How do I know that my employees are getting what they expect from the company? You'll be able to tell if your employees are happy with what they are receiving by their attitude towards work. If you see employees who are generally happy at their posts, and who do not complain about their compensation on a regular basis, you can be relatively sure that your employees are happy with what they are receiving. On the other hand, if you see employees who drag their feet, are grumpy, and who complain about their paychecks and benefits you likely have a workforce that does not feel the company is meeting their expectations.

To meet your employees' expectations there are a few steps you can take.

How to meet employee expectations is 3 steps.

1.) **Review:** Look at the benefits packages you provide and determine if there are areas that you could improve i.e. pay increases, bonuses, better health benefits, etc.
2.) **Reward:** Try to implement a benefits system that allows employees to pick and choose various rewards to allow for a customized package to appeal to the individual expectations of each employee.

3.) Revise: Ask for suggestions from your employees, listen to what they have to say, and implement as many changes as you can. This gives employees a sense of ownership in the company.

Example

One day a manager notices that one of her employees is slouched at his desk, with his hand on his chin, and elbow on his desk. She decides to go up to the employee and say," Hi Jared, how's it going today?"

"Fine," Jared replies unenthusiastically while looking down at his desk.

"You look like you might be a little bit upset." The manager says while looking empathetically at Jared.

"I'm just a little worried about my wife, and the baby." Jared says as he looks up at the manager.

"Why's that?" The manager asks. "Are they okay?"

"Well, my wife is pregnant, and our health insurance doesn't cover the delivery costs. I don't know how I'm gonna pay the bill."

"Oh, I'm sorry about that, but we only have one insurance option that we provide." The manager says looking down as she has heard this complaint many times before.

"I just feel like I should be able to get better health benefits for the work that I do." Jared says looking at the manager.

"I wish there were something I could do for you. Sorry I can't help." The manager says as she begins to walk away.

Do you think Jared is getting what he expects from the company? Not really. He feels as though he should be able to have more options in his health coverage due to the amount of effort he puts forth in his job. The manager feels bad about the situation, but does not offer any solutions.

What could she do? At times managers may not be able to help employees, but in this situation the manager could've suggested that she would request a meeting with human resources and the insurance provider to see about getting some more options available to employees. Even if she wasn't able to come through with more options she at least would have shown Jared that she values him as an employee, and that his efforts are appreciated. Sometimes employees are motivated because they know their managers genuinely care for them even if they can't get everything they want.

Tip: Try to understand how your employees feel about the compensation they are receiving. On a regular basis, praise employees for doing good work, and let them know they are appreciated.

Adam's Equity Theory

The equity theory revolves around the idea that employees will attempt to maintain an equilibrium between what they put into their work, and what they get out of the company.[15] This means that employees feel that the requirements of their job are equal to the compensation their company is providing. This is determined by a sense of fairness between what each employee receives. Employees compare fairness by looking at their coworkers to conclude that the compensation provided to each individual is equal. If they feel that there is an imbalance between what one worker receives to the next they will be unhappy with their individual compensation.

Equity theory is more about equal compensation for all employees than it is about individual effort. Individual effort is important in that employees who do not perform at the same level as their coworkers should not receive the same compensation, but should have the opportunity to be rewarded in the same manner as everyone else. The compensation anticipated is the same as that of expectancy theory (pay, benefits, time off, supervisor recognition, etc.).

This theory is built on three assumptions. The first assumption is that employees expect to receive compensation for their effort that is equal to the rewards provided to everyone else. This means that employees feel that they are receiving the same amount of reward as the worker next to them. This notion leads to the second assumption, employees judge the level of fairness, or equality, by looking at what workers around them are receiving. If workers notice an imbalance in the compensation provided to some employees as opposed to others, they will feel that an inequality exists, and will be unmotivated to put forth their best efforts. The third assumption is that employees are able to create an equitable situation by changing their input into the company and by changing the rewards provided. If employees feel that an inequality exists in compensation they have the ability to bargain with their companies to change the compensation packages they are receiving. This allows them to gain a sense of equality in what each employee is receiving.

The most common place equity theory is found today is within Unions. The goal of a Union is to protect workers' rights, and make certain that workers receive fair compensation for the work they are providing to companies. If the union feels that there is an inequality in the rewards provided to employees they will negotiate with company leaders to create a more equitable situation. This ensures that each union member will receive equal compensation for the effort they put into the company.

Unions can be beneficial to employees in that they can rest assured they are being treated the same as the worker standing next to them. Union members benefit from knowing that their pay, benefits, and time off are the same as everyone else around them. This concept allows employees to feel that their compensation is equal to their effort.

How do I know if my employees feel that the rewards provided are equal? You will only be able to know if employees feel they are being treated equally if you ask them. As a manager you can ask them directly to give their opinions about how they perceive the compensation packages your company provides. Workers often don't get to see the process company leaders go through to create compensation packages, and may have many misunderstandings about how rewards are decided upon within your organization.

Make sure that you are getting candid, and honest, responses from employees. You may need to bring in an outside source, such as a consultant, to help gather unbiased opinions. Workers may feel pressured to tell their manager that they are more positive about their working conditions than they genuinely feel. A consultant will be able to elicit responses that are less biased as he or she will have no influence over the employees, and will be able to explain why honest responses are beneficial to everyone. Once the consultant has compiled the responses he or she will report the findings to you, and make suggestions on how to improve employees' feelings of equity.

Once you have gained an understanding of your employees' feelings about the company you can take a few steps to help employees feel more equitable in your company.

How to improve equity and meet employee expectations in 4 steps.

1.) **Explore:** Look at your compensation packages and decide if there are any ways to make them more equitable.
2.) **Explain:** If you find areas that can be improved upon, create a presentation to explain to the employees any changes you are thinking about implementing. Be as transparent as you can with explaining the process of determining compensation packages.

3.) **Examine:** Ask for employee feedback to check if your changes will help them feel that the compensation packages are equal amongst each other.

4.) **Execute:** Implement as many changes as you can to help employees feel equal. This will empower them by giving them a sense of ownership in how they are treated by the company.

Tip: Implementing change is not always feasible in company budgets or resources. If big changes will require a significant cost, try to come up with ideas of smaller changes you can implement to show your employees that they are appreciated. This will go a long way in helping to keep your workforce motivated.

Which Theory?

The main difference between the two theories is that equity theory focuses on the equal compensation of members of a group where expectancy theory focuses on the rewards provided for individual effort. They are similar in that employees expect to be compensated for their effort, and if employees feel they are not receiving fair compensation they will not be motivated to do anything more than the minimal amount necessary to keep their jobs. Understanding which theory is most prominent in your organization is vital to understanding how to implement motivation strategies.

Motivation for workers will be similar in many ways, but needs to be tailored to the belief system of your employees. Neither theory is better than the other for employee motivation. The difference rests in the hands of management's understanding of employees' beliefs, and their ability to implement motivational techniques.

Where does motivation come from?

Motivation is a characteristic of human behavior that is apparent in all aspects of our lives. We are motivated to get up, get dressed, and go to work. We are motivated to eat, drink, and be merry. We are motivated to seek out relationships with other people. We are even motivated to be sad at times. Motivation is the reasoning behind all our behaviors.[16]

Think about a child in line at the grocery store screaming for a piece of candy. What is the parent doing? The parent is likely quickly scrambling to give the child the candy she wants. The motivation for the parent to give the child the candy is to get her to stop crying, and avoid an embarrassing scene in public. This seems like a reasonable response. However, what is the motivation of the child to cry? The child is motivated to cry for the candy simply because she wants it. Through her experiences she has learned that if she cries the parent will give her what she wants. This is the reasoning behind her crying, or the origins of her motivation.

It is not fair to compare employees to children, but the concept is the same. Employees expect to receive rewards for their work. Companies provide rewards to employees for the effort they contribute to the organization. If the rewards provided by a company are valuable to employees, they will be motivated to put forth their best effort to get them.

What are valuable motivators to employees? All motivation can be broken down into one of two categories which are internal motivation, and external motivation. A researcher by the name of Abraham Maslow created a hierarchy of needs that describe internal and external motivations. This theory is built on the understanding that humans have basic external needs of survival (food, shelter, and water), and internal needs (love, recognition, and security).[17] Maslow believed that as one need was met the next became more important. Refer to *figure 3*.

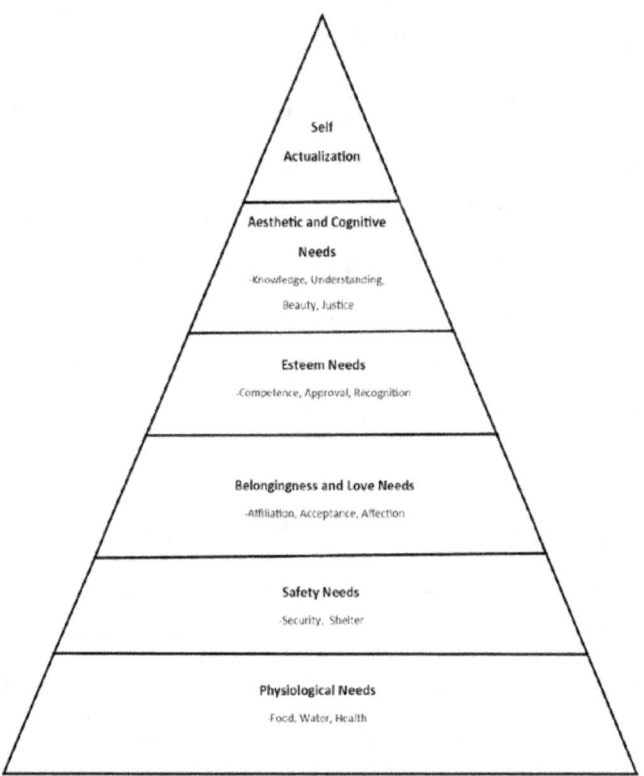

Figure 3 Maslow's Hierarchy of Needs

Maslow's theory is important in understanding the two categories of motivation because it explains why certain aspects of the workplace have value for employees. Let's explore the two types of motivation and why each is important.

Internal Motivation

The first type of motivation focuses on the internal beliefs of individuals. Every human being has thoughts and feelings that are unique and personal. These thoughts and feelings influence the decisions people make regarding what behaviors to display. As thoughts and feelings influence people's behavior they become motivators for specific actions. If a person feels happy inside they may express that happiness outwardly by smiling and laughing. The individual may not be aware that he or she has chosen to display this behavior, but their internal feelings motivated an expression of how they are feeling in a public manner. This would be a subconscious reaction to an internal motivation.

A conscious reaction to an internal motivation may be telling someone you love them because you feel it in your heart. This is conscious because you have thought about this action, and decided that speaking out publicly to the person you love is the right choice. Your motivation was to express your internal feelings of love to let the other person know how you feel.

In a work environment I wouldn't recommend going around telling people you love them but, the concept applies to motivation at work in the same manner. Employees are motivated to perform based on their thoughts and feelings about their job, compensation, and workplace. Each employee needs to make decisions about how to behave at work based on his or her internal beliefs. An employee who feels good about his or her job will likely have a higher level of internal motivation than an employee who has negative feelings towards the work environment.

Internal motivators.

What motivates someone internally? As mentioned earlier the thoughts and feelings of humans are unique to each individual. Internal motivation is no different. Motivators that are important to one individual may not be as important to another. Here is a list of a few internal motivators that influence the level of motivation employees express.

Acceptance: The feeling of being accepted into a group is a strong motivator for many people. People join groups and teams to fulfill their need of being accepted. Employees who do not feel they are accepted as a member of a company are not likely to be motivated workers. Employees who are able to feel as though they have been accepted into an organization and are welcome will show higher levels of motivation. Helping employees to feel accepted in your company will prove to be a valuable tool in your motivational strategy. Most employees will naturally get to know their coworkers as time passes, but if you notice a new employee feeling left out try to encourage him or her to talk to coworkers and get to know them. You may need to introduce the new worker to other employees to start conversations.

Affection: When you look at a 6'3", 300-pound, bearded man you might think that he does not have any emotions, or that they are limited to simple, Neanderthal like, feelings. This is a stereotype that many people believe, which is wrong. This man is just as sensitive as everyone else. Every human being has a need to feel affection. This is the motivation behind seeking out relationships and working hard to keep them. The workplace may not seem appropriate to display affection, but if done properly can be a strong motivator. Simple acts such as a fist bump can be a display of affection that does not imply any notion other than management cares about the employees. Also, greeting an employee on his or her birthday can be a sign that the manager cares enough to remember. Finding simple acts of affection to show your employees that you care about them as individuals will go a long way in motivating them. Most people tend to leave out this section due to the potential for controversy. Though showing affection in the workplace can be risky, if done properly it can also be a powerful motivator for individuals.

Warning! Be sure that the acts of affection you are showing your employees are appropriate, and that they do not overstep any boundaries that make employees feel uncomfortable. The point is to let them know you care about them without crossing any inappropriate lines.

Knowledge: People have a natural need to learn new things. Some more than others but, everyone enjoys learning something new. Most people won't spend their free time studying mathematical equations, but may read articles on fishing, cars, sports, hairstyles, clothes, etc. Learning in the workplace can be a strong motivator for many employees in that with new knowledge comes new responsibilities. Many employees are looking for opportunities to learn new skills to further their careers. Providing training opportunities for employees to learn new skills is a powerful motivator that can be implemented in many ways. You can hold formal meetings to share new ideas with employees. Send employees to training seminars. Encourage employees to take courses in specific areas of business that you think they will enjoy, and that will benefit your company. You can also personally teach new skills to employees, or bring in an outside trainer.

Recognition: Most employees have a desire to be recognized, and appreciated for their efforts. No one likes to work hard for a company they feel does not appreciate them. Recognizing your employees' efforts both formally and informally is a powerful tool to provide motivation to your team.

Informal recognition comes in the form of saying, "Good job on these reports." Or, saying, "These parts look great." You can say these types of praises to your employees privately, just you and the employee, or publicly where other workers hear you say them. Employees like social recognition from their coworkers just as much as they like it from you the manager.

Formal recognition may come in the form of an engraved plaque that signifies a special achievement that an employee has accomplished. You can have a small gathering of coworkers, or a large gathering of employees to recognize the achievements in a formal manner. This is a useful tool in your motivational strategy as it empowers employees to take pride in their work, and to take ownership of their responsibilities within the company.

Tip: Design your motivational strategy to include each of these internal motivators. As a general rule the motivator you use most often is recognition because it can be applied at any given time. Make every effort to recognize the achievements of your employees both big and small. The more you're able to show your appreciation to your employees the more motivated they will be to produce high-quality work.

External motivation

What motivates someone externally? External motivators are outside of our thoughts and feelings and influence our physical well-being. Employees need to feel comfortable with their surroundings, and know that their external needs will be met by their companies. Here are a few examples of external motivators.

Food and water: Food and water are strong motivators for people. Today in America we don't often think about how important access to food and water is until an emergency arises. When a disaster strikes people are not worried about entertaining themselves by going to the cinema. They're worried about how they will find enough food and water to sustain the lives of their children and themselves. In the workplace the way you are able to meet the need for food and water of your employees is by providing a consistent place to work. Employees are motivated by the knowledge that they will have a job tomorrow so that they can feed their families. Providing a level of job security to employees goes a long way in your motivational strategy without the need to talk about it with your employees on a regular basis. However, if something comes up in your business that might affect your employees' job security, being transparent will help them to cope with any changes that are necessary. Don't hide information that could affect their livelihoods from your employees.

Physical safety: We all have a natural instinct to feel secure in every environment in which we find ourselves. We want to feel safe in our homes, in the grocery store, and at our places of employment. Safety is a big concern for workplaces and over the past several decades has gained the attention it deserves. Workplaces around the world are implementing more safety standards than ever in history. At times, you will hear employees complain about safety standards but, when you ask them," Do you feel safe in the workplace with these safety standards?" Most employees will say that the safety standards do make them feel secure, but may be slightly inconvenient to deal with on a daily basis. Even if the safety standards are slightly inconvenient for employees they will be motivated to feel safe and secure in their workplace by the procedures you implement. This supports their overall motivational level by knowing that they can go to work and return home every day. Ensuring that your company implements the latest and most effective safety standards is a strong tool in your motivational strategy.

Pay: If you ask 1000 people why they go to work they will tell you they go because they need money to take care of their families, or live their lives. Money is a powerful motivator of humans. Paying employees is one of the most important aspects of business operation. Employees need to feel comfortable with the level of pay they receive for their work, to be motivated to put forth their best efforts. As we saw in expectancy theory and equity theory employees have a level of expectation for the amount of compensation they will receive compared to the amount of effort they put forth. Deciding upon how much to pay your employees requires careful consideration. Many factors influence your ability to pay, your perception of what employees deserve for their work, and the perception of what the employees feel they deserve. Try to always provide a level of payment that is acceptable to everyone involved. Paying employees is the foundation of your motivation strategy. If you're able to pay employees a wage that is more competitive than other companies, do so. If you're not able to pay them above the normal rate, at least pay them the average wage for their particular position. Help employees understand why they are paid the amount you are giving, and help to motivate them utilizing methods mentioned earlier.

Tip: Make every effort to pay your employees as well as you possibly can. Their paycheck is a powerful motivator as they see it every week, two weeks, or month. It is a powerful motivator because they will feel internally rewarded by seeing the value of their effort, and feel externally motivated by having the money they need to satisfy their physical needs.

How to motivate employees in 4 steps

To motivate employees, you need to design a motivational strategy that you can implement at any given time. This will involve deciding upon which motivational characteristics are the most important to your workplace. Using the internal and external motivational factors mentioned earlier, you can pick and choose which areas are the most import for you personally based on your knowledge of the employees working at your company. Once you have decided upon the most important elements of motivation you can design a strategy that allows you to be able to quickly and easily use motivational techniques on a daily, weekly, monthly, and yearly basis.

> **1.) Daily:** Motivational techniques allow employees to be constantly aware of your appreciation for their hard work. These techniques do not require a great deal of time to implement each day, but do require consistency. If you give positive comments every day for two weeks, then every other day for a week, and then randomly here and there employees will

not be able to feel the constant appreciation that you want to provide them. You do not need to complement every employee every day just make sure that in a rotational manner you get to praise all your employees for their efforts. Don't leave anyone out.

2.) Weekly: Choose an employee each week who has done a great job, and praise him or her in front of all of his or her coworkers. This provides a great incentive for people to work hard to receive public recognition for their efforts. As mentioned earlier, people are motivated by social recognition as much as by recognition from their supervisor.

3.) Monthly: Choose an employee each month who has worked hard and shown a great deal of progress over the past few weeks. Again, it is a great motivator to socially recognize employees in front of their peers. You can provide them with a certificate of achievement, or some other incentive such as a gift card, to further motivate employees to strive to be chosen as the employee of the month.

4.) Yearly: Take the time to recognize an employee who has not only demonstrated to you that he or she deserves special recognition, but also has gained in the admiration and respect from his or her coworkers. Take into account suggestions made by your employees for selecting an employee of the year to help instill ownership among the employees, which motivates them all to give their best effort to the company. Also, the recipient of the employee of the year award is highly motivated by recognition given by supervisors as well as the knowledge that coworkers recognize his or her effort in providing high quality work.

Here is an example.

My Motivational Strategy

Daily

Find one or two positive comments I will say to employees privately or in front of co-workers. Praise employees for all good work I see completed. Encourage employees to keep up the good work.

Weekly

Recognize an employee every week in front of all of his or her co-workers for doing a great job.

Monthly

Choose an employee of the month who has done exceptional work.

Yearly

Ask employees to vote on an employee of the year, and have a ceremony to celebrate.

Figure 2 My Motivational Strategy

Tip: Design a strategy that is most effective for your workplace based on your employees' feelings about expectancy, and equity. Take all of these factors into consideration and design a strategy that allows you to cover as many motivational areas as possible. This will help your employees to be constantly aware of your appreciation for them.

Take away

Expectancy theory – employees believe that the harder they work the greater the rewards they will receive.

Equity theory – employees compare their rewards to those of their coworkers.

Internal motivators – thoughts and feelings about factors that influence the level of motivation of employees such as affection, knowledge, and recognition.

External motivators – factors outside of a person that influence his or her level of motivation such as food and water, pay, and shelter.

Creating a motivational plan will help you to continuously motivate your employees on a daily, weekly, monthly, and yearly schedule.

Chapter 7

Delegating responsibility

How can I be effective at delegation?

Surround yourself with the best people you can find, delegate authority, and don't interfere.

- ***Ronald Reagan***

Managers are responsible for many tasks. Some of these tasks are essential to the manager's role and should not be given to anyone else. However, many tasks that a manager finds him or herself completing could easily be passed on to an employee. The manager does not typically need to be the one sending faxes, filling the coffee pot, or loading paper into the printer. These may seem like trivial tasks, but for a manager time is a limited commodity. Filling up your day with small tasks takes away time from completing more important projects. To become the most efficient manager learning to delegate responsibility will help you to eliminate tasks from your schedule that are taking up your time. Once you understand the power of delegation you will be able to free up more of your time to focus on the important aspects of your job.

What does delegating responsibility actually mean? Delegation is assigning tasks that managers are responsible for to employees. The employee will take on the task and complete it, but the manager remains ultimately responsible for the work. This allows managers to focus their time on more important duties while still ensuring that all the tasks are being completed. Delegating effectively maximizes the manager's ability to successfully complete all of his or her duties.

To learn to effectively use delegation start by creating a list of all the tasks you complete in a given day, week, and month. Go through your list and prioritize your duties into three categories: essential, semi-essential, and non-essential.

Essential tasks - include job duties that you must complete yourself and should not be assigned to anyone else.

Semi-essential tasks - are tasks that have importance but could be completed by someone else if needed.

Non-essential tasks - are all the small tasks that do not need to be completed by a manager in any way.

Once you've identified and prioritized your tasks find all the nonessential tasks that take up your time. Many of these tasks will be able to be eliminated entirely because they are not needed. Other nonessential tasks you will be able to eliminate by assigning to your employees. There is no problem with the manager who takes responsibility and fills in gaps where needed, but being responsible for higher-level tasks as well as low-level tasks consumes too much of the managers time.

How to delegate responsibility in 5 steps

Once you've decided to delegate responsibility you will need to begin the process of selecting someone to complete these tasks. To delegate effectively you can follow this five-step plan.

1.) **Analyze:** First, take a look at the list of tasks you have created. Identify the semi-essential tasks. Look through this list and determine if any of these tasks are getting in the way of completing your essential tasks. If semi-essential tasks are blocking you from focusing on your essential tasks you will need to delegate these to an employee.

2.) **Select:** Next, think about your employees and create a short list of people who could possibly take on the tasks you are delegating. Think about their strengths, weaknesses, and knowledge. Refer to

Chapter 5 for identifying employee strengths. Once you have identified employees look at their schedules to see if they will be able to add more responsibility to their workload. Give the employee sufficient time to complete the task you will be assigning to him or her.

3.) Define: Once you've selected an employee to take on one of your tasks you must provide a clear explanation of what is expected of him or her. The task you are assigning may be semi-essential to you, but may be completely new to the employee. You need to clearly communicate to the employee all the aspects of the task you are assigning. You want your employee to feel comfortable taking on this added duty and avoid causing him or her unneeded stress.

4.) Monitor: As the employee takes on the responsibility you will need to ensure that he or she is completing the task as you have asked. You can do this by providing support to the employee, and encouraging the employee to come to you with questions. Be available to answer their questions to help them feel more comfortable. Also, provide feedback to employees as they complete different sections of the task. Be encouraging and supportive of the tasks they've completed correctly, and be gentle with correcting their mistakes. This is a new process for the employee and may take a little time to learn. Finally, empower the employee by allowing him or her to work without your guidance. This is a great tool for employee motivation.

5.) **Review:** The last step in the delegation process is to provide a final performance review of the employee. This is a chance for you to praise the employee for taking on more responsibilities, completing new tasks, and learning new skills. Providing positive feedback to employees about a job well done helps to motivate them, and gives them a sense of pride in their work. For more on employee motivation refer to *Chapter 6*.

Using this method, you will be able to effectively and efficiently delegate responsibility to your employees. Doing so will allow you to free up time for more important aspects of your job.

Tip: An added benefit of delegation is that you provide new experiences to your employees, and allow them to grow in their jobs. This helps to motivate them and may increase their loyalty to the company. The benefits of delegation greatly outweigh the risks.

Example

After another long, hard, week you decide to take a look at your schedule and see if there's anything you can eliminate. You make a list of tasks and prioritize them as essential, semi-essential, and non-essential. You start to look at the non-essential tasks and eliminate some of these from your schedule. Other nonessential tasks need to be completed, but not by you. You start thinking about who could take on these tasks without putting too much pressure on them. You come up with a short list of people who could take on some of these simple tasks.

Then you move on to looking at your semi-essential tasks. You see that one of your tasks is creating a quarterly report for the Board of Trustees. You decide that this report takes up a great deal of your time because it involves organizing pieces of information in a document, and requires proofreading and editing. You decide that this task could be given to one of your employees as long as you are able to keep watch over its progress. You start to look at your employees and determine who would be able to take on the added responsibility.

You decide on two employees who would be good at completing the quarterly report. You take a look at their schedules and see that one of them has tasks that require more time than the other. So, you choose the employee who has a little bit more flexibility in scheduling. You approach the employee and ask her if she would like to take on some additional responsibility and assist you with the quarterly report. The employee agrees, and you begin teaching her all the skills needed to properly compile the report.

As time goes on, you check in with the employee to see how she is progressing, and check to see if any support is needed. If she has any questions you answer them, and teach the proper way to complete each task involved with the report. As she gets better at the skills you check in less, and allow her to take responsibility for the report.

Before the report is due you have the employee submit it to you for final review. You praise her for learning new skills, taking on added responsibility, and a job well done. You thank her for the effort and let her know that you appreciate her hard work.

Take away:

Following this five-step method will help you become efficient at delegation.

Analyze – determine which tasks you can delegate to others.

Select – choose the right employee to take on the responsibility.

Define – clearly explain the requirements of the task.

Monitor – support the employee and provide feedback to their questions.

Review – provide a final performance review to the employee praising them for a job well done.

Chapter 8

Managing Change

How do I manage change effectively?

> Management's job is to see the company not as it is...but as it can become.
>
> — attributed to **John W Teets**

Change is a part of life that no one can escape. Change occurs around us constantly and is necessary for growth. When you are a child you regularly learn new concepts and change the way you think. When you're a teenager you begin to have unique thoughts and feelings that will shape who you will become. As an adult you grow from your experiences and change your perspective on how you view life. Times of change can be quite scary, but can also be exciting. The opportunities that change brings can be worth the stress and anxiety that come along with the change process. However, we tend to focus on the negative risks that could be associated with change. Even though the potential for positive results can be exhilarating it is difficult for some people to look past the potential for negative consequences. As a manager it is up to you to help make sure that everyone involved is able to clearly see what will come from the changes.

Companies have no chance of survival without changing from time to time. You can hardly walk into a business today that does not use a computer system. The introduction of computers into the business world changed how businesses around the globe operate. Those who were able to quickly adapt computer technology were more likely to stay at the top of their fields. Those who were slow to incorporate computer technology had much more catching up to do. Fear of introducing new technology held many companies back from being able to keep up with the times in new technology.

This concept is true also for communications and marketing. Communication technology has evolved by leaps and bounds in the past two decades. It has changed the way people connect with each other, no matter where they are in the world. Marketing has also changed. With the advent of the Internet, more and more companies focus marketing budgets to online ads and social media content. Marketing budgets used to be comprised of primarily intrusive techniques such as billboards, radio commercials, and television ads. Now marketing focuses more on relationship building sales through online content. Companies who were able to adjust to these new marketing techniques have been able to reach more clients than ever. The Internet is connected to the entire world, and allows people from all corners of the earth to freely communicate with each other.

These types of changes have been difficult for many companies, but have provided them with opportunities to grow their business and become more successful. Changes in technology, communication, and marketing are all types of anticipated changes that companies need to be ready to tackle. Unanticipated changes are much more difficult to plan for, but with consideration into the aspects of successful change management companies will be ready to meet any challenge they may face.

Anticipated changes

Success lies in the ability of companies to change. Many changes can be expected and planned for by anticipating what will be required to successfully implement the coming adjustment. As I mentioned earlier, many changes can bring about new opportunities for the growth of businesses. Planning for these changes in advance will help you to successfully navigate the change process and reduce the negative consequences that could be associated with making changes.

Several aspects of business are known to change on a regular basis. Let's explore a few.

Technology: No one can deny that technology has changed the face of the business environment around the world. More business can be conducted on a cell phone today then could have been done with an entire office 30 years ago. Technology has helped many businesses become much more productive and efficient. Keeping up to date with technology helps businesses to stay with the times and reach potential clients who utilize new technologies every day.

Look at Facebook. A college kid in his dorm room decided to create a website that students at Harvard University could log onto and rate how good-looking their classmates were.[19] People on college campuses quickly began using Facebook to communicate socially. It grew from one campus to the next and exploded from there. In a period of just a few years Facebook went from an idea in a dorm room to a social media phenomenon that is now worth multiple millions of dollars. Businesses all around the world invest significant portions of their marketing budgets into creating Facebook pages, campaigns, and advertisements. Even politicians use Facebook to connect with potential voters because they know that millions of people can be located in one spot with just a few clicks of the mouse.

Many businesses today are run solely on the Internet without the need for any true physical location other than a chair, an internet connection, and a laptop. Small business owners, especially, are able to reduce costs by eliminating high rental prices for offices. The advantage technology brings to these companies is that they can be much more efficient in smaller spaces than ever before. Many people earn a good living by staying at home and earning money online.

Anticipating the need to change how you use technology can be the difference in the ability of your company to continue on a path of growth. Being reluctant to learn about new technology and the advantages it can have for your business will only result in your company being left behind. Not all technology will benefit your company's needs, but there is no question that your company will need to continuously improve its use of technology to stay competitive.

Tip: Learning new skills associated with technology can cause fear in many people. To curb this fear provide enough time to train your employees so they feel comfortable with new technologies.

Communication: The flow of information in a company from top executives down to entry-level employees plays a vital role in the overall functioning of any business. The more clarity people have in communication, the more likely they will be at understanding where the company is and where the company needs to go. Communication technology has helped improve this process over the last several years. Just 20 years ago the most effective means to communicate an idea to everyone within the company was a memorandum. Many of you remember these, but for those who don't it was essentially a letter written to employees to inform them of information they needed to know. The memos were printed out and delivered manually to each employee who needed a copy. This took time, effort, and money to print enough memos to supply everyone with the information. The memorandum concept improved the ability of companies to transfer information to many people at the same time, but had its drawbacks. At times people would either lose memos or they would not be delivered. This left gaps in information for many people. There is a common saying," Didn't you get my memo?" This used to be a common phrase around offices. Now you would hear," Didn't you get my e-mail?"

    E-mail, or electronic mail, has changed the way people use written communication. E-mail is essentially a free way of presenting information to as many people as necessary. It is also an instant form of communication in that as soon as you press the send button the e-mail reaches the inboxes of an unlimited number of recipients. You can spend 10 minutes writing one e-mail and send it to 100,000 people. Mere seconds after you send the e-mail it will pop up in recipients' mailboxes and be available for them to read. This has not only changed the way businesses operate locally, it has effected business internationally. The company needing to send information to Japan can write an e-mail and rest assured that in a few seconds the e-mail will be available for the reader on the other side of the world. This used to take many days for a written letter to be delivered. E-mail technology has allowed companies to become more efficient at communicating information than ever before.

  The same concept is true with telephone communication. Cell phones today can be carried in your pocket and brought with you, no matter where you go, even to foreign countries. I remember thinking how amazing it was that as I stood on the Great Wall of China I could call my mother and brothers in America and wish them a happy new year.

  Cell phone technology allows companies to connect with employees, and customers no matter where they are. As long as an employee has his or her cell phone turned on he or she can be reached without the need to pull off at a gas station to find a pay phone. This allows companies to quickly and efficiently transfer information that employees need to know as soon as possible.

Keeping up to date with communication technology will help your company to be productive and efficient. This is a vital aspect in your company's ability to meet the needs of the times and remain competitive. The investment required to continuously update communication technology may be expensive, but the ability to communicate efficiently is far more valuable.

Tip: Not everyone in your company will need a cell phone but, if you see that providing cell phones to some key employees will help productivity don't be afraid to make the investment.

Growth: Another type of change that can be anticipated is future growth of your company. If you plan to expand the reaches of your organization to new markets, a plan for managing the change process will be an invaluable tool. Creating a plan for growth helps you see roadblocks that will come up and address them before they are reached. Also, creating a detailed growth plan will help you anticipate changes needed in personnel, technology, marketing, and communications. The greater effort you put into anticipating these changes, the more likely you will be at creating a successful path for growth.

Tip: If you're planning to grow your company start with creating a one year, five year, and 10 year plan. Then make a detailed list of all the changes you will have to implement to achieve your goals. Create detailed plans for each change process as they will make the transition much smoother.

Unanticipated changes

Despite your best efforts to plan for change there will inevitably be times when changes are thrust upon you without your choice. These are situations in which you have no control other than how you will face them. Later in this chapter we will discuss how to create a system for meeting anticipated and unanticipated changes. For now, let's look at a few unanticipated changes.

Economy: Only a handful of people around the world have any true influence on the economy. These are typically world leaders and high-ranking politicians. The rest of us are subject to economic tides that can either bring great prosperity or bring financial ruin.

In 2008, as the American economy plummeted the economies of countries around the world also fell. I was living in South Korea at the time and being paid in Korean won. Before the economy crashed the exchange rate of Korean won to US dollars was very good for me. Over the period of a couple of weeks the exchange rate began to turn, and the value of the US dollar fell to a point where I was losing 50% of my income to the exchange rate. A 50% reduction in my paycheck was extremely difficult for my family. But, what could I do? I had no choice but to tighten my belt and cut back on everything I possibly could. Nothing I could do would improve the economy.

As I faced this challenge I realized that a significant change in my income had a drastic effect on my livelihood, but I did not let it defeat me. I learned to create more efficient plans for the money I was receiving and to keep myself motivated by focusing on the fact that the economy would improve over time. This concept is applicable to every company. Though drastic changes may be thrust upon you being able to weather them without giving up hope will be the difference between your company being successful, or failing.

Tip: If you will be working overseas, always get paid in American dollars. I learned this the hard way. If I had been paid in American dollars the exchange rate would've allowed me to increase my salary by 50% rather than decrease.

Markets: Depending on the markets in which you operate, changes in market conditions happen on a daily basis. One day you could be overrun with orders where you are thinking about hiring new people to meet the demands.

The next day orders can be canceled, and you could be contemplating laying people off. As an individual manager, you have no control over specific market conditions. The only thing you can control is how you will meet these challenges. Having a contingency plan in place will allow you to meet market demands, and have a safety net to fall back on in case business slows down.

Tip: If at all possible, set aside enough resources to keep your business running for six months to a year. This will give you a safety net to fall back on in tough times.

Natural disaster. If we could predict natural disasters countless lives, and businesses, could be saved. Unfortunately, there is no possible way of predicting accurately when natural disasters will occur, or how much damage they will cause. Hurricanes, tornadoes, volcanoes, earthquakes, and tsunamis are a fact of life on planet Earth.

I saw firsthand the devastating effects that natural disasters can have after Hurricane Katrina. I went with a group to Pass Christian, Mississippi to help with the recovery effort. While there I saw homes and businesses completely destroyed. We drove past a Walmart and all that remained was a spiderlike skeleton of the building. Everything inside the store was completely washed out. Behind the store was a line of trees that was completely covered in Walmart bags 30 feet in the air. We also drove past what used to be a bank. All that was left was a concrete slab and a gigantic steel safe, the rest of the building was gone.

Preparing to deal with natural disasters can be the difference between recovering and failing. Dealing with disasters can be devastating to companies, but with a disaster preparedness plan companies may be able to remain in business while recovery efforts are taking place. I once toured the headquarters of a nationwide insurance company. The company's headquarters was located in an area that was prone to have tornadoes. When this company decided to build their headquarters in this location they took into consideration what a tornado would do to the structure. They built the walls with reinforced concrete to ensure that they would not be blown down, and they built in a double roof system. If a tornado hit the building and tore off one roof another roof was in place underneath it to keep the building protected.

Not all companies will be able to have such elaborate buildings designed, but having a plan to outsource aspects of your business in times of need will assist you in meeting these challenges if they come up.

Tip: To create a disaster preparedness plan prioritize the functions of your business and build relationships with companies who can help you meet these needs. For example, having a relationship with a company that rents temporary office space is a good idea if your building is damaged, so that you will have a place to move your operations.

How to manage change with 5 skills.

Whether changes are anticipated or unanticipated your ability to navigate the change process will be dependent on your ability to lead. Napoleon Bonaparte said, "A leader is a dealer in hope."[20] Change can be frightening for many people, and can lead to stressful situations. As a manager, your job is to lead your employees through the process with the least amount of resistance possible. Employees may resist change, and fight for their ability to remain in their comfort zone. Your job is to help them see outside of their comfort zone and realize the potential positive, or negative effects that change will bring.

To manage change leaders must invest in their ability to plan for leading employees through different aspects of the change process. To do so managers need to focus on five key areas.

> **1.) Effective communication:** The ability of managers to transfer information to everyone involved in the change process is the most

important aspect of managing change. Effective communication allows everyone involved to understand what is happening, why it's happening, and why the change is important. Whether it is anticipated or unanticipated, communicating effectively to your employees will be the difference between smoothly transitioning, and going through a rough change process.

Why is communication so important to the change process? Communication is the building blocks of effective business. No one likes ambiguity when it comes to change. Everyone involved wants to have all information available. Communicating to your employees as much information as possible will help eradicate resistance to change. As employees understand the stages in the change process they will be much more likely to meet challenges with open arms. They may not like to be put in a change scenario, but with effective communication they will be able to understand why each step is necessary. Becoming the most effective communicator that you are capable of will help you face changes with certainty and confidence.

Tip: The more you know about the change process the more your employees should know. Make every effort to keep everyone involved and as informed as possible. Don't keep people waiting for information. Step up your communication efforts to make certain that everyone involved is as comfortable with the change as possible. For more on effective communication refer to *Chapter 2*.

2.) Motivation: As we explored in *Chapter 7*, motivation plays a significant role in your employees' ability to be successful in their jobs. During times of change ensuring that your workforce is motivated can significantly reduce the negative aspects of the change process. Employees who are motivated will continue to produce high-quality work. If you allow your workforce to become de-motivated through the change process they will be less likely to meet the challenges of change. The more enthusiastic you can make your employees the more likely you will be at successfully managing the change process.

Why is motivation important? The morale of your employees will make all the difference in their acceptance of change. Employees who have high morale will look at changes as being positive and bringing about opportunities for growth. Employees with low morale will not likely put forth effort to make changes successful because they may not understand the importance of making changes for the success of your company. If you are able to clearly communicate to them why changes are necessary, and motivate them to put forth enough determination to tackle each stage in the change process, you will be able to lead your company to positive results.

Unfortunately, not all changes are positive. At times companies have no choice but to reduce their workforce. This does not go over well with most employees. In these times motivating your employees will be very challenging, but the more effort you put into keeping morale high, the smoother the transition will be for you and the employees.

Tip: If you're facing a positive change in your organization, but fear you will meet resistance, get creative with your motivational strategies. Try something new that will excite your employees. For example, arrange an extended lunch period for employees and have a barbecue. Or, treat your employees to a day at the ballpark. Allowing your employees to have social interaction on company time can have a significant impact on their level of motivation.

> **3.) Managing stress.** Stress is another one of those unavoidable aspects of life. Though we cannot escape stress we can learn to effectively manage how we let stress affect our well-being. Times of change within companies can be quite stressful on everyone involved. Employees may be stressed about the potential negative consequences of change. Managers may be stressed by the pressure felt from their employees. To successfully manage

change you must understand how stress affects you as well as how it affects your employees.

How do I reduce my stress? Stress is only as powerful as you allow it to be. If you allow stress to consume your life it can cause severe implications to your health. Emotional stress can make you physically ill. To combat this, you must believe that you are stronger than your stress, and that you have the power to control how stress affects you. Once you believe that you have power over your stress there are several techniques that can help you to attack stress as it approaches. Here is one technique for reducing your stress.

Find a quiet place where you can be alone for a few minutes.

Make the environment as relaxing as you can. If this means closing blinds, or lowering lights do so.

Close your eyes and begin a breathing pattern of 5 seconds in, and 5 seconds out. (If 5 seconds is too long reduce it so that it's comfortable for you.)

As you are breathing, think about a time when you achieved something great i.e. winning a trophy, or being recognized for your hard work.

Try to remember all the positive feelings you had at that time.

Once you've gone through that memory open your eyes and notice the difference in your stress level.

This is a technique you can use almost anywhere. Once you become familiar with this technique you will be able to use it very quickly to help escape from stressful situations for a few minutes. Escaping from your stress, even for a few minutes, helps you significantly reduce the amount of negative consequences that stress has on your body and mind.

How do I reduce employee stress? Employee stress is different than your own because it is not practical to have all of your employees sit in a quiet place and go through the technique mentioned earlier. Unless you have a smaller workforce, or a small team, that would benefit from such a technique. The most effective means to help manage stress across all your employees is to communicate as effectively as possible, and to continue to encourage motivation among your workers. The more informed employees are about the change process the less stress they will encounter. It's up to you to keep employees informed and keep them motivated to reduce their level of stress.

Tip: Another useful tool to reduce stress is simply to laugh. Find something that makes you laugh and allow yourself to fully engage in laughter. Laughter frees up serotonin in your brain which helps you feel more positive.

4.) Teamwork: Teamwork is an important aspect of most businesses. This is never more apparent than in times of change. The better your teams are at working together to accomplish goals the more likely they will be able to meet the challenges of change and overcome. As a manager, emphasize the importance of teamwork to continuously motivate your teams to produce the highest quality results.

Why is teamwork important? Teamwork plays a pivotal role in the ability of companies to meet challenges. Teams are able to bounce ideas off each other and come up with creative solutions to problems that would be much more difficult to accomplish individually. Utilizing the ability of your teams to be creative will help alleviate a significant amount of stress and confusion. Make sure to reinforce the idea that teams = success to your employees, and encourage them to grow closer as a team. For more on teams see *Chapter 5*.

Tip: Team building exercises are a great way to help your teams become closer so that they can work together in a more efficient manner. In times of change get creative with team building exercises to help members overcome any challenges they may have with working together successfully.

5.) Get help: The change process can be very stressful for everyone involved. Sometimes the added requirements of managing change may be too much for one person, or team, to handle. In these situations, calling in help from outside sources may be the best choice you could make for the success of your project. Hiring a consultant may significantly help implement change as consultants may have the skills and experience necessary with specific areas of change that you are trying to confront. Consultants can help alleviate the pressure on everyone involved by taking on a large portion of the responsibility for ensuring that the change process is moving forward. This can significantly increase the ability of projects to be successful.

When hiring a consultant take into consideration the cost of his or her services. Weigh the cost of the services against the value that a consultant can bring to your project. If the value significantly outweighs the costs, move forward in selecting a consultant. Don't let the financial cost of a consultant hold you back from seeking his or her help. The return on investment for hiring a consultant can be 10x the financial cost of adding him or her to your team.

Tip: Consultants can be found in almost every field of business. Choose a consultant who has the knowledge necessary to help you with your specific tasks.

Example

I used to be a social worker and worked with adults with developmental disabilities. One day in our office someone approached me and said that the state was cutting funding to social service programs, and that he heard our company was going to be laying off people. I was the newest hire at the time and immediately felt worried about my job. I was not the only one who was scared though. Everyone in the office was worried that we would all be laid off and be unemployed by the end of the month.

When we found out about this we went to our manager and asked her if she had any information. She informed us that she did not know if the budget cuts would affect us or not. In the two weeks following this news we anxiously awaited new information from the state to trickle down to our organization. During this time my manager kept reassuring us that she was doing everything she could to find out more information. She called several state agencies to see if they could give her any concrete facts about what the budget cuts would effect. Every time she called a state agency she would let us know what she learned, if anything at all. She made every effort to keep us informed as new details emerged. To help keep us motivated she arranged a day where we could all bring in a dish and have a potluck for lunch. It may not seem like much, but it was a great way for all of us to unwind and alleviate some stress. After about two weeks we learned that the budget cuts were not going to affect our organization. We were all very relieved to know that we were going to keep our jobs.

This was an unanticipated change. No one knew for sure if the changes to the state budget were going to affect our office or not. Although no actual changes occurred during this process for my office, the stress of the situation was no less than any other change scenario. My manager was able to reduce our stress by keeping us informed of information she learned. Also, she was able to keep all the employees motivated by arranging a social activity for us to bond and forget about our worries, even if only for a short period of time.

Take away:

Whether a change is anticipated or unanticipated the manager's role is to effectively lead employees through the entire change process. To do so managers need to be effective at five skills.

Effective communication – keep employees informed of all aspects of the change process as soon as information is available.

Motivation – keep your employees motivated as their morale will make all the difference in change success.

Manage stress – strive to eliminate as much stress from your life as possible, and alleviate employee stress by keeping them informed and motivated.

Teamwork – continuously emphasize the importance of teamwork for the success of project goals.

Get help – don't be afraid to seek outside assistance with projects. Look for consultants who can help you achieve your goals.

Chapter 9

Conflict resolution

How do I effectively resolve conflicts?

The ultimate measure of a man is not where he stands in moments of comfort, but where he stands in times of challenge and controversy.

– Dr. Martin Luther King Jr.

Conflicts inevitably come up when people interact with each other. It seems to be human nature that people will disagree on pretty much every issue possible. We face conflicts in our daily lives and react to them in various ways. Conflicts arise not only in our personal lives but at work as well. Conflict in the workplace can cause stress and negativity to the point where business is interrupted. Workplace conflict can revolve around racial discrimination, gender discrimination, age discrimination, differences of opinion, or be as simple as what type of coffee to buy for the break room.

Conflicts large and small affect companies. There is no getting around the fact that conflicts get in the way of conducting business. However, conflicts do not have to destroy relationships. They can be met with professionalism and acceptance. As a manager you will need to become proficient at resolving conflicts. If you can master the skill of resolving conflict, you'll be able to help create a positive workplace that is built on mutual respect and trust.

Conflicts are going to arise, but resolving them respectfully, quickly, and appropriately will have an impact on all of your employees. Resolving conflicts is a task that leaders must take on to mediate the effects conflicts will have on everyone involved.

How to resolve conflicts in 5 steps

Each conflict is unique in who is involved, why it came about, and how it can be appropriately resolved. No matter the unique characteristics of a disagreement, following this five-step plan will allow you to successfully resolve conflicts.

1.) **Congregate:** The first step in conflict resolution is to bring all the parties involved together in a private room. Only include the individuals who were directly involved in the conflict, yourself, and another supervisor if necessary. Do not involve witnesses to conflicts unless the matter is of a grave nature such as discrimination, harassment, or abuse. For all other conflicts stick to just the people involved.

2.) **Communicate:** Once you've gathered everyone involved into a private place allow each person to tell his or her side of the story. As each person is describing the situation encourage them to focus on what the other person in the conflict was feeling rather than what that person was thinking. Many times, conflicts can be resolved by helping parties acknowledge the other person's feelings as opposed to what they imagine the other person was thinking. Acknowledging feelings helps people to connect with others, even when they have a disagreement. Allow each person to fully express their feelings about the situation.

3.) **Validate:** By helping employees focus on the feelings of the other person involved in the conflict you will be able to encourage them to validate each other's unique perspective. This means that you encourage employees to look at the situation from the other person's point of view, and try to understand why the other person has those feelings about the situation. Validating everyone's feelings helps ensure that a resolution is possible as everyone involved in a conflict wants to be heard and acknowledged.

4.) Negotiate: The fourth step in the conflict resolution process is to negotiate a solution to the problem at hand. To successfully negotiate conflicts, ask each person involved to suggest a solution to the problem. After you've gathered the opinions of the employees, offer your suggestions as well. Once you've got a list of possible solutions determine a way to combine them so that each of the people involved feels that they have been heard, and that they feel comfortable with the solution you are suggesting. Each person needs to feel that they have been treated respectfully and professionally throughout the conflict resolution process.

5.) Motivate: The final step in the conflict resolution process is to encourage employees by helping them understand that conflict is a natural part of human life. Also, help them understand that if conflict is resolved appropriately there is almost always a chance to learn something new. Do not view conflicts as failures, view them as opportunities to grow. Encourage your employees to learn from these experiences, and to grow as unique individuals.

Tip: If you come across a small conflict you may not need to have such a formal process. If you come across employees arguing over which coffee to make in the break room, follow the five-step plan but do so while standing near the coffee machine. This process does not have to be lengthy or drawn out. It can be done in a quick and efficient manner once you have mastered the skill.

Example

One afternoon you're sitting at your desk answering e-mails and you hear a shout come from across the office. You get up to investigate, walk out of your office, and ask the first person you see about the shouting. You get some direction and walk over to find a female worker crying in her hands. You ask her what happened, and she informs you that her male coworker yelled at her when she asked a question.

What do you do?

First, congregate the parties involved. Ask the female worker and the male worker to accompany you to your office.

Second, communicate by allowing each to tell his or her side of the story.

Third, validate by encouraging both employees to acknowledge the other person's feelings.

Fourth, negotiate by asking each employee to offer a solution to the conflict.

Fifth, motivate employees to show more respect to each other and to learn from this experience.

Following these five steps will allow you to quickly navigate through the conflict resolution process.

Here is an example dialogue of how this scenario could have happened.

The manager is sitting at her desk typing e-mails and hears a shout. She gets up to investigate and finds a female employee, Joan, crying in her hands.

Manager: "What's wrong Joan?"

Joan: "Josh shouted at me when I asked him a question."

Manager: "I'm sorry that he shouted at you. Why don't you go down to my office and wait for me there?"

Manager: "Hi Josh, Joan told me that you shouted at her. Is that true?"

Josh: "Yeah it's true. I didn't mean to do it, but I did shout at her."

Manager: "Why don't we go down to my office and we can all talk about it?"

Manager: "Now that we're all here let's close the door and talk about this. Joan why don't you start by telling me what happened. When you talk about Josh try to think about what he was feeling at the time this was all going on."

Joan: "Okay, I was sitting at my desk when I saw Josh walk up and I knew I needed to ask him about the marketing report. I asked him if he would have it done today or not, and he shouted at me saying, "I'm not finished yet." He said it in such a hurtful way and shouted at me. I couldn't help but cry. I guess he was feeling frustrated about not having it done and he took it out on me."

Manager: "Thanks for sharing that Joan. I understand that it was hurtful to be shouted at and probably embarrassing too. Now Josh, why don't you tell me what happened from your perspective. Remember to think about what Joan was feeling while this was all going on."

Josh: "I have been under a lot of pressure lately to finish the marketing report, but I have been held up because I'm waiting on information from other departments. This morning I had a fight with my wife before I came to work, and I have been a bit wound up all day. When John asked me about the marketing report I just sort of snapped and shouted at her. I can understand how she would feel very upset about the way I reacted to her. I feel really bad about it and I'm sorry."

Manager: "Okay, I can see how you'd be frustrated with the marketing report and not having all the information you need. Also, I understand it's difficult sometimes when you're thinking about personal issues while at work. I know that you would not intentionally hurt Joan's feelings and that you sincerely regret what happened. Joan, what do you think an appropriate solution to this situation would be?"

Joan: "I can see that he didn't mean to upset me and all I need is an apology."

Manager: "Do you agree with the solution Josh?"

Josh: "Yes, of course I do. I am very sorry for the way I treated you Joan. You did not deserve to be yelled at no matter what my personal issues are. Will you accept my apology?"

Joan: "Yes, I accept your apology. Thank you for being sincere."

Manager: "I understand this was embarrassing for both of you, but don't be discouraged. Learn from this experience and remember to do your best and always be courteous and respectful of each other. Josh, if you're feeling upset about something, practice some stress reducing techniques. If you need help with this let me know and we can discuss ways to help you alleviate your stress. Even though you are upset about something at home be sure that you remember to be respectful of your coworkers. Does everyone feel comfortable with resolving this issue?"

Joan: "Yes, I do."

Josh: "Yes, I do too, and again I'm sorry."

Manager: "Okay, let's go back to work now. Let's just keep the shouting to a minimum this time, okay?"

The two employees leave with a smile on their face.

In this example we can see how the manager congregated employees, communicated their feelings about the situation, validated their feelings, negotiated a solution, and motivated the employees to learn from the experience.

Take away:

Conflicts will inevitably arise. How you handle conflicts as a manager will define your leadership abilities. To resolve conflicts efficiently follow this five-step plan:

Congregate – gather all parties involved together.

Communicate – allow each person involved to express their feelings while thinking about what the other person was feeling during the situation

Validate – encourage everyone involved to acknowledge the feelings of the other people even if they disagree.

Negotiate – ask each person involved to offer a resolution to the problem and come up with a solution that is acceptable to everyone.

Motivate – encourage employees to learn from the situation and grow as individuals.

Chapter 10

Firing

Who do I fire, and how do I do it?

You're fired!

— Donald Trump

      Firing employees is the most dreaded aspect of management for most people. Not very many managers will tell you that they enjoy firing people. Those who do say they enjoy it are quite likely the Competitor, and they relish in the power that firing people has over their lives. Most managers would rather do pretty much anything than fire someone. At times managers don't fire someone simply to avoid the conflict. These are generally the Avoider or the Accommodator type managers. No matter which type of manager you are, you need to come to an understanding that at times some employees will need to be let go. You may make every effort possible to help them keep their job, but some employees will have a negative influence that is too great to overlook.

As a manager you have an ethical obligation to make every effort to know that your employees are safe and secure in their jobs. However, your responsibility is also to the company. If an employee is negatively influencing the entire company, or department, you may have no choice but to fire him or her. If after several attempts to correct the employee's behavior he or she is still not performing appropriately you must make a decision about his or her future with the company.

How to fire someone in 4 strategic stages

The ability to fire someone is a necessary aspect of the manager's responsibilities. To be effective at firing employees, managers need to be able to make decisions that are free from personal emotion, and that are the best choices for the overall good of the company. To discern that you're making the right choice to fire someone here is a four-step plan you can follow.

1.) **Analyze:** The first step in the process in firing someone is to analyze the situation. In this step you will determine who needs to be fired and why. To do so, think about the problem employee. Ask yourself a series of questions to decide if the employee should continue working, be retrained, or be fired from your company.

What are the problem behaviors of this employee?

Are the behaviors serious enough to fire this person?

Could these behaviors be corrected with training?

Could these behaviors be overlooked?

What is the overall positive effect this employee has on the company?

What is the overall negative effect this employee has on the company?

Will the company be a stronger place without this employee?

Are the behaviors of this employee damaging business or hurting the company's reputation?

Once you've compiled your answers to these questions look at the total amount of positive answers compared to the total amount of negative answers. If the positives are markedly stronger than the negatives you can choose a course of action to help keep this employee on your staff. If the negatives outweigh the positives you will need to consider firing this employee. This leads us to step two.

2.) **Prioritize:** Now that you have an idea of whether to pursue firing an employee you must make sure that your decision is in the best interest of your company. Look back at the positive to negative ratio you created in step one. Determine a global positive effect for the employee, and a global negative effect. A global effect is the overall influence an employee has over the success of your company. A global positive effect will include all the constructive aspects an employee brings to the organization. The global negative effect includes all the negative aspects the employee brings to the job.

If the negative global effect is hurtful to your company the employee needs to be fired. Employees who damage the business of your company, or its reputation, should be let go. The overall well-being of your company, as well as the well-being of your other employees, is more important than one individual.

3.) **Authorize:** Once you come to a decision to fire an employee you need to review your decision. It is important that your decision is based on the goal of the overall well-being of the company, not based on your personal feelings about the situation. When firing someone make every effort to leave your emotions out of the situation. This can be very difficult, but ensures that you are making decisions based on what is best for everyone else involved.

Before you authorize an employee to be fired, take time to clear your head and get away from the situation for a while. Clearing your mind of the situation will help you to come back to it with fresh eyes, and confirm that you are making the right choice. Do something that will allow you to fully detach yourself from the situation for a long enough period that you can focus on something else.

For example, if you decide to fire someone Thursday afternoon go home and watch a movie that night to escape from thinking about the situation. In the morning, go back to work and look at the situation again. If you still agree with your decision from the day before you will know that it is the right decision for your company.

> **4.) Finalize:** The final step in the firing process involves ratifying the decision you've made. When you bring the employee into your office remember to be firm but fair. Be sure to be respectful throughout the process, and explain to them why you have come to the decision to fire them. If you cannot give them a good explanation as to why they are being fired, you have not properly prepared for this stage. You should be able to give them a list of

points that fully explain why the employee is no longer needed.

Once you've explained to them why they're no longer needed, ask if they have any questions. Give them instructions regarding how you would like them to exit the company, and when the final work day will be, if other than immediately. Shake their hand as they leave and wish them the best.

Tip: Always be respectful to employees even if they are being fired for a good reason. Showing respect helps your employees respect your decision.

Example

For several weeks you been receiving complaints from coworkers and customers about Jordan. You have made several attempts to help Jordan change his behaviors. He has been unresponsive to your suggestions and his work is affecting your business. Coworkers feel uncomfortable around him, and feel he is not contributing to the team.

After the attempts to correct Jordan's behavior have failed you decide to analyze the situation. Make a list of questions (see step one) and compile a list of answers based on the information you've been given by coworkers and customers. Next, prioritize the situation by counting the number of negative responses you gave to the answers in your questions, and count the number of positive responses. This gives you a ratio of positive to negative responses from which you can create a global positive effect and a global negative effect that Jordan is having on your company. Now move to authorize the decision to fire Jordan based on the fact that his global negative effect greatly outweighs his global positive effect on the organization. You have taken time to relax and spent an evening watching a movie at home. The next morning you have come back to the office and reviewed the information you created the day before. You decide the global negative effect is still stronger than the global positive affect and that there is no more room in your organization for Jordan. You call Jordan to your office and release him from the company.

The conversation may go like this:

Manager: "Jordan will you please come to my office?"

Jordan: "Sure I'll be right there."

Manager: "As you know Jordan there've been many complaints about you lately. I've tried to discuss a few options for improving your work performance, but I have not seen enough of a change to show me that you genuinely care about your job here."

Jordan: "So, what are you trying to say?"

Manager: "I'm saying that you are no longer needed for your position here, and I'm letting you go. The complaints against you are affecting business as customers feel you are unresponsive to their requests. Also, many of your coworkers do not feel that you are contributing to the team and are uncomfortable working with you. You have not shown me a desire to improve upon these aspects through the conversations we've had over the last several weeks. For these reasons I am releasing you from the company."

Jordan: "I don't agree with you. I think I have been doing a good job, but my coworkers all team up against me."

Manager: "I'm sorry you feel that way Jordan, but it's not just the complaints from your coworkers that have led me to this decision. I took all the information I had into careful consideration and weighed each piece on multiple occasions. This was not an easy decision, but I feel it is best for the company. Do you have any questions?"

Jordan: "Well, I'm sorry you feel that way. What will I do now?"

Manager: "I'm sorry as well Jordan, I wish you the best of luck in finding a company that will be a good fit for you. Please leave your badge at the front desk when you leave on Friday."

Jordan: "Is there anything I can do to stay here?"

Manager: "I'm sorry Jordan, you have been given several opportunities to improve and you didn't show many signs that you wanted to keep this job. I must make decisions that are best for the company and the other employees who work here. Take this experience with you to your next job and remember to take your manager's suggestions into consideration when they give you an opportunity. I really do wish you the best. Take care."

The manager clearly went through the reasoning behind firing Jordan. The manager explained to Jordan why the decision was made while still showing him respect. The manager was firm about his decision and did not change his or her mind when Jordan requested to stay. The manager treated Jordan fairly by explaining that he had been given several opportunities to improve, but Jordan chose to continue his negative behaviors. This resulted in a professional and respectful firing process.

Take away:

Firing employees may be one of the most difficult aspects of the manager's responsibilities but, with a four-step strategy you will be able to efficiently decide who should be fired, and how to do it.

Analyze – compile a list of questions and answers to identify positive and negative aspects of an employee's performance.

Prioritize – create a global positive and global negative effect that the employee has on the company. If the global negative effect is greater than the global positive effect the employee will need to be terminated.

Authorize – carefully consider your decision to fire an employee, and take time to leave the decision until you can come back to it with fresh eyes.

Finalize – be firm, but fair with employees showing them respect at all times. Explain to them why they're being fired and allow them to ask any questions. Wish them the best of luck, and instruct them on how to leave the organization.

Appendix – Systems

How to improve your speaking abilities in 5 Steps

1.) **Write.** Write down all the areas in your work life in which you need to use verbal communication. These will include having conversations, giving presentations, and praising your employees.
2.) **Think.** Think about how you would approach each of these situations and what you might say. Is there a better way to say it? Can I improve the amount of time I spend in each of these areas if I reorganize how I am saying this?
3.) **Implement.** Apply the skills learned in written communication to your speaking. Ask yourself am I being clear in what I'm saying? Am I being concise? Is what I'm saying professional? This will help you eliminate a significant amount of unnecessary words. Also, remember to speak in a natural manner that reflects how you normally talk. Don't forget to slowdown. Rushing leads to misunderstandings.
4.) **Strategize.** Create a set of strategies you can use to assist you in utilizing these new speaking skills.
5.) **Practice.** Practicing speaking will help you grow in your ability as well as your confidence. The more you practice the better you will become, and the more

comfortable you will feel with speaking in all types of situations.

How to improve work ethics in 4 steps.

1.) Ask: Ask yourself whether any parts of your work make you uncomfortable? Then ask yourself why you are uncomfortable with these parts of your work life?

2.) Develop: Develop a set of personal ethical standards that you can apply to your work. You can create a list based on your personal beliefs according to religion, world views, and life choices.

3.) Compare: Look at your list and compare it to your company's formal policies, as well as the unwritten rules at your workplace. Often workplaces have a set of unwritten guidelines that workers are expected to follow. Compare your personal ethical standards and determine if they align.

4.) Implement: If they do align you are good to go. Just think about ethical choices when difficult situations arise. If they do not align, you may have to rethink your career path, or attempt to create changes in your workplace.

How to conduct interviews in 4 Phases.

1.) **Introduction phase:** This is the first encounter you have with the candidate in person. When they come into the interview room greet them by shaking their hand and welcoming them to the interview. In this phase it is important to help the candidate feel comfortable and relaxed. Interviews can be very stressful for people. Some people may be fantastic at their job, but have a hard time with the pressure of interviews. To help alleviate the stress begin by asking some personal questions of a friendly nature such as," Did you find the building okay?" After they answer that question ask them something else such as, "Are you originally from this area?" Asking these types of questions allows candidates to alleviate some of their stress by focusing on something unrelated to making a good impression on a potential new boss. This allows them to ease into the interview process and relax before you begin the Q&A phase.
2.) **Q&A phase:** During this phase of the interview process you will be asking the candidate questions to determine if they will be a good fit for your company. You can do this by studying their resume and asking them questions about the experiences

they've had, their education, and any gaps in information you notice on the resume. Keep the Q&A phase structured, but allow for a bit of flexibility as well. This will help keep the interview rolling in a smooth fashion.

3.) **Investigation phase:** Design your questions based on the strategy you have decided upon, and have a prepared list of questions to ask the candidate before they arrive at the interview. Use your list to cover the information necessary to determine if they will be a good fit, but be flexible so that you can add in questions you notice about answers the candidates provide. Follow-up questions may lead to a significant amount of information that you would not have otherwise learned. Depending on the strategy you are utilizing, ask questions based on specific situations, facts, and technical knowledge necessary for the job. Asking a series of investigative questions will help you conclude if they not only have the necessary skills, but also the personality traits to best fit your organization.

4.) **Wrap up phase:** After you've gotten all the information you need from a candidate open the floor to the candidate to ask questions he or she may have about the job. Encourage the candidate to ask as many questions as they need to feel comfortable even if you have already decided that they will not be a good fit for your company. The last thing you want to do is make a candidate feel bad about the interview. Also, if you are feeling like the candidate may be a good fit allowing them to ask questions may help support your instinct to hire this person. This allows the candidate to gain a more comprehensive picture of what will be required of him or her, as well as to gain further knowledge about what the job will entail. Once all the questions are finished stand up, shake the candidate's hand, and thank him or her for coming to the interview. Standing up shows the candidate that the interview is over and that they are free to go.

How to pick teams in 6 steps

1.) **Decide:** You must decide if the team will be led by you, or as a self-managed team. If you will be leading a team you already have one of the six members. If you are not leading the team yourself, you'll need to choose a team leader from your employees.

2.) Create: Create a description of the project, or permanent structure, for which you need a team and make a list of the skills, knowledge, and personality traits necessary.

3.) List: Make a list of your employees by classifying them into one of the six categories above: the leader, the implementer, the thinker, the contributor, the builder, and the inquisitor.

4.) Explore: Look at the personality traits of your employees and determine if they will be able to work together well on a team. Take note of any office conflicts that have arisen in the past, and try to avoid putting coworkers together who have personality clashes.

5.) Select: From the employees you have who meet the requirements select members to fill each of the roles.

6.) Inform: Notify employees that you would like them to join a team, let them know why they have been chosen, and what their role will be on the team.

How to meet employee expectations is 3 steps.

1.) Review: Look at the benefits packages you provide and determine if there are areas that you could improve i.e. pay increases, bonuses, better health benefits, etc.

2.) **Reward:** Try to implement a benefits system that allows employees to pick and choose various rewards to allow for a customized package to appeal to the individual expectations of each employee.

3.) **Revise:** Ask for suggestions from your employees, listen to what they have to say, and implement as many changes as you can. This gives employees a sense of ownership in the company.

How to improve equity and meet employee expectations in 4 steps.

1.) **Explore:** Look at your compensation packages and decide if there are any ways to make them more equitable.

2.) **Explain:** If you find areas that can be improved upon, create a presentation to explain to the employees any changes you are thinking about implementing. Be as transparent as you can with explaining the process of determining compensation packages.

3.) **Examine:** Ask for employee feedback to check if your changes will help them feel that the compensation packages are equal amongst each other.

4.) **Execute:** Implement as many changes as you can to help employees feel equal. This will empower them by giving them a sense of ownership in how they are treated by the company.

How to motivate employees in 4 steps

1.) **Daily:** Motivational techniques allow employees to be constantly aware of your appreciation for their hard work. These techniques do not require a great deal of time to implement each day, but do require consistency. If you give positive comments every day for two weeks, then every other day for a week, and then randomly here and there employees will not be able to feel the constant appreciation that you want to provide them. You do not need to complement every employee every day just make sure that in a rotational manner you get to praise all of your employees for their efforts. Don't leave anyone out.

2.) **Weekly:** Choose an employee each week who has done a great job, and praise him or her in front of all of coworkers. This provides a great incentive for people to work hard to receive public recognition for their efforts. As mentioned earlier, people are motivated by social recognition as much as by recognition from their supervisor.

3.) **Monthly**: Choose an employee each month who has worked hard and shown a great deal of progress over the past few weeks. Again, it is a great motivator to socially recognize employees in front of their peers. You can provide them with a certificate of achievement, or some other incentive such as a gift card, to further motivate employees to strive to be chosen as the employee of the month.

4.) **Yearly:** Take the time to recognize an employee who has not only demonstrated to you that he or she deserves special recognition, but also has gained in the admiration and respect from his or her coworkers. Consider suggestions made by your employees for selecting an employee of the year to help instill ownership among the employees, which motivates them all to give their best effort to the company. Also, the recipient of the employee of the year award is highly motivated by recognition given by supervisors as well as the knowledge that coworkers recognize his or her effort in providing high quality work.

How to delegate responsibility in 5 steps

1.) **Analyze:** First, take a look at the list of tasks you have created. Identify the semi-essential tasks. Look through this list and determine if any of these tasks are getting in the way of completing your essential tasks. If semi-essential tasks are blocking you from focusing on your essential tasks you will need to delegate these to an employee.
2.) **Select:** Next, think about your employees and create a short list of people who could possibly take on the tasks you are delegating. Think about their strengths, weaknesses, and knowledge. Refer to *Chapter 5* for identifying employee strengths. Once you have identified employees look at their schedules to see if they will be able to add more responsibility to their workload. Give the employee sufficient time to complete the task you will be assigning to him or her.
3.) **Define:** Once you've selected an employee to take on one of your tasks you must provide a clear explanation of what is expected of him or her. The task you are assigning may be semi-essential to you, but may be completely new to the employee. You need to clearly communicate to the employee all the

aspects of the task you are assigning. You want your employee to feel comfortable taking on this added duty and avoid causing him or her unneeded stress.

4.) Monitor: As the employee takes on the responsibility you will need to ensure that he or she is completing the task as you have asked. You can do this by providing support to the employee, and encouraging the employee to come to you with questions. Be available to answer their questions to help them feel more comfortable. Also, provide feedback to employees as they complete different sections of the task. Be encouraging and supportive of the tasks they've completed correctly, and be gentle with correcting their mistakes. This is a new process for the employee and may take a little time to learn. Finally, empower the employee by allowing him or her to work without your guidance. This is a great tool for employee motivation.

How to manage change with 5 skills.

1.) Effective communication: The ability of managers to transfer information to everyone involved in the change process is the most important aspect of managing change. Effective communication allows everyone involved to understand what is happening, why it's happening, and why the change is important. Whether it is anticipated or unanticipated, communicating effectively to your employees will be the difference between smoothly transitioning, and going through a rough change process.

2.) **Motivation:** As we explored in *Chapter 7*, motivation plays a significant role in your employees' ability to be successful in their jobs. During times of change ensuring that your workforce is motivated can significantly reduce the negative aspects of the change process. Employees who are motivated will continue to produce high-quality work. If you allow your workforce to become de-motivated through the change process they will be less likely to meet the challenges of change. The more enthusiastic you can make your employees the more likely you will be at successfully managing the change process.

3.) **Managing stress.** Stress is another one of those unavoidable aspects of life. Though we cannot escape stress we can learn to effectively manage how we let stress affect our well-being. Times of change within companies can be quite stressful on everyone involved. Employees may be stressed about the potential negative consequences of change. Managers may be stressed by the pressure felt from their employees. To successfully manage change you must understand how stress affects you as well as how it affects your employees.

4.) **Teamwork:** Teamwork is an important aspect of most businesses. This is never more apparent than in times of change. The better your teams are at working together to accomplish goals the more likely they will be able to meet the challenges of change and overcome. As a manager, emphasize the importance of teamwork to continuously motivate your teams to produce the highest quality results.

5.) **Get help:** The change process can be very stressful for everyone involved. Sometimes the added requirements of managing change may be too much for one person, or team, to handle. In these situations, calling in help from outside sources may be the best choice you could make for the success of your project. Hiring a consultant may significantly help implement change as consultants may have the skills and experience necessary with specific areas of change that you are trying to confront. Consultants can help alleviate the pressure on everyone involved by taking on a large portion of the responsibility for ensuring that the change process is moving forward. This can significantly increase the ability of projects to be successful.

How to resolve conflicts in 5 steps

1.) **Congregate:** The first step in conflict resolution is to bring all the parties involved together in a private room. Only include the individuals who were directly involved in the conflict, yourself, and another supervisor if necessary. Do not involve witnesses to conflicts unless the matter is of a grave nature such as discrimination, harassment, or abuse. For all other conflicts stick to just the people involved.

2.) **Communicate:** Once you've gathered everyone involved into a private place allow each person to tell his or her side of the story. As each person is describing the situation encourage them to focus on what the other person in the conflict was feeling rather than what that person was thinking. Many times, conflicts can be resolved by helping parties acknowledge the other person's feelings as opposed to what they imagine the other person was thinking. Acknowledging feelings helps people to connect with others, even when they have a disagreement. Allow each person to fully express their feelings about the situation.

3.) Validate: By helping employees focus on the feelings of the other person involved in the conflict you will be able to encourage them to validate each other's unique perspective. This means that you encourage employees to look at the situation from the other person's point of view, and try to understand why the other person has those feelings about the situation. Validating everyone's feelings helps ensure that a resolution is possible as everyone involved in a conflict wants to be heard and acknowledged.

4.) Negotiate: The fourth step in the conflict resolution process is to negotiate a solution to the problem at hand. To successfully negotiate conflicts, ask each person involved to suggest a solution to the problem. After you've gathered the opinions of the employees, offer your suggestions as well. Once you've got a list of possible solutions determine a way to combine them so that each of the people involved feels that they have been heard, and that they feel comfortable with the solution you are suggesting. Each person needs to feel that they have been treated respectfully and professionally throughout the conflict resolution process.

5.) **Motivate:** The final step in the conflict resolution process is to encourage employees by helping them understand that conflict is a natural part of human life. Also, help them understand that if conflict is resolved appropriately there is almost always a chance to learn something new. Do not view conflicts as failures, view them as opportunities to grow. Encourage your employees to learn from these experiences, and to grow as unique individuals.

How to fire someone in 4 strategic stages

1.) **Analyze:** The first step in the process in firing someone is to analyze the situation. In this step you will determine who needs to be fired and why. To do so, think about the problem employee. Ask yourself a series of questions to decide if the employee should continue working, be retrained, or be fired from your company.
- What are the problem behaviors of this employee?
- Are the behaviors serious enough to fire this person?

Could these behaviors be corrected with training?

Could these behaviors be overlooked?

What is the overall positive effect this employee has on the company?

What is the overall negative effect this employee has on the company?

Will the company be a stronger place without this employee?

Are the behaviors of this employee damaging business or hurting the company's reputation?

Once you've compiled your answers to these questions look at the total amount of positive answers compared to the total amount of negative answers. If the positives are markedly stronger than the negatives you can choose a course of action to help keep this employee on your staff. If the negatives outweigh the positives you will need to consider firing this employee. This leads us to step two.

> **2.) Prioritize:** Now that you have an idea of whether or not to pursue firing an employee you must make sure that your decision is in the best interest of your company. Look back at the positive to negative ratio you created in step one. Determine a global positive effect for the employee, and a global negative effect. A global effect is the overall influence an employee has over the success of your company. A global positive effect will include all the constructive

aspects an employee brings to the organization. The global negative effect includes all the negative aspects the employee brings to the job.

If the negative global effect is hurtful to your company the employee needs to be fired. Employees who damage the business of your company, or its reputation, should be let go. The overall well-being of your company, as well as the well-being of your other employees, is more important than one individual.

> **3.) Authorize:** Once you come to a decision to fire an employee you need to review your decision. It is important that your decision is based on the goal of the overall well-being of the company, not based on your personal feelings about the situation. When firing someone make every effort to leave your emotions out of the situation. This can be very difficult, but ensures that you are making decisions based on what is best for everyone else involved.

Before you authorize an employee to be fired, take time to clear your head and get away from the situation for a while. Clearing your mind of the situation will help you to come back to it with fresh eyes, and confirm that you are making the right choice. Do something that will allow you to fully detach yourself from the situation for a long enough period that you can focus on something else.

For example, if you decide to fire someone Thursday afternoon go home and watch a movie that night to escape from thinking about the situation. In the morning, go back to work and look at the situation again. If you still agree with your decision from the day before you will know that it is the right decision for your company.

> **4.) Finalize:** The final step in the firing process involves ratifying the decision you've made. When you bring the employee into your office remember to be firm but fair. Be sure to be respectful throughout the process, and explain to them why you have come to the decision to fire them. If you cannot give them a good explanation as to why they are being fired, you have not properly prepared for this stage. You should be able to give them a list of points that fully explain why the employee is no longer needed.

Once you've explained to them why they're no longer needed, ask if they have any questions. Give them instructions regarding how you would like them to exit the company, and when the final work day will be, if other than immediately. Shake their hand as they leave and wish them the best.

Review Request

Thank you for reading *Management, How to*. I hope you enjoyed reading it as much as I enjoyed writing it. If you did enjoy it, please help me out by leaving a review on Amazon that expresses what you got from reading this book.

Thank again for reading *Management, How to*. I wish you the best in your adventures in management.

References

1. Tzu, S., & Giles, L. (1910). *The Art of War.*

2. Abraham Lincoln Online. (2012). *Abraham Lincoln Political Career Timeline.* Retrieved from Abraham Lincoln Online: http://showcase.netins.net/web/creative/lincoln/education/polbrief.htm

3. McGregor, D. (2000). The human side of enterprise. *Reflections.*

4. Homer. (n.d.). *The Iliad, Book XIV, Line 251. Pope's Translation.*

5. Anthony, S. (2012, April 10). *The history of supercomputers.* Retrieved from Extreme Tech: http://www.extremetech.com/extreme/125271-the-history-of-supercomputers

6. Fox News. (2013, April 03). *The mobile phone call was placed 40 years ago today.* Retrieved from Fox News: http://www.foxnews.com/tech/2013/04/03/first-mobile-phone-call-was-placed-40-years-ago-today/

7. History. (2013, June). *Ronald Reagan.* Retrieved from History.com: http://www.history.com/topics/ronald-reagan

8. Dumbrava, G., & Koronka, A. (2009). Actions speak louder than words - Body language in business communication. *Annals of the University of Petorsani, Economics, 9*(3), 249-254.

9. The Walt Disney Company. (2013, April 2). *Eeyore.* Retrieved from Facebook: https://www.facebook.com/WinniethePoohEeyore

10. Mankiewicz, J. (2006, November 7). *For Politicians, the gesture's the thing*. Retrieved from NBC News: http://www.nbcnews.com/id/15609023/#.UVsHqxzlaDk

11. Lincoln, A., & Basler, R. P. (2008). *The Collected Works of Abraham Lincoln edited by Roy P. Basler, Volume IV, "Remarks at Painesville, Ohio", (February 16, 1861)*. Wildside Press.

12. Thoreau, H. D., & Suba, S. (2010). *Life without principle*. Kessinger Publishing, LLC.

13. The TQM Magazine. (1995). What is a team? *The TQM Magazine, 7*(3), pp. 62-63.

14. Eerde, W. V., & Theirry, H. (1996). Vroom's expectancy models and work-related criteria: a meta analysis. *Journal of Applied Psychology, 81*(5).

15. Huseman, R. C., & Hatfield, J. D. (1990). Equity theory and the managerial matrix. *Training and Development Journal, 44*(4).

16. Vallerand, R. J., & Lalande, D. R. (2011). The MPIC model: the perspective of the hierarchical model of intrinsic and extrinsic motivation. *Psychological Inquiry, 22*(1), 45-51.

17. Maslow, A. H. (1943). A preface to motivation theory. *Psychometric Medicine*, 85-92.

18. Fortune Magazine. (1986, September 15). Making, planning, Gorbachev, and more. *Fortune*.

19. Facebook. (2013, April 5). *History of Facebook*. Retrieved from facebook:

https://www.facebook.com/pages/History-of-Facebook/105185536206799#

20. Bonaparte, N. (1916). *In his own words: Edited by Jules Bertaut, as translated by Herbert Edward Law and Charles Lincoln Rhodes.*

21. King , M. L. (2010, 1963). *Strength of love.* Minneapolis, MN: Fortress Press.

22. NBC. (n.d.). *The Apprentice.* (D. Trump , Performer) Retrieved from www.nbc.com/the-apprentice